The ascent of Japanese
companies boosting
management through
brand power

Branding
WORLD-
BEATING
Companies

imajina, inc.
Yoshiki Sekino
[President and CEO]
Yumiko Okuyama
[CCO (Chief Culture Officer) and Managing Director]

世界で勝てるブランディングカンパニー

ブランド力でマネジメントを強化する日本企業の挑戦

株式会社イマジナ　代表取締役社長・関野吉記／代表取締役・奥山由実子

ダイヤモンド社

ブックデザイン
森田恭行
髙木瑶子(キガミッツ)

世界で勝てるブランディングカンパニー

Branding WORLD-BEATING Companies

目次

08 はじめに

[特別インタビュー]

16 世界を勝ち抜いていく
ジャパン・ブランドの「鉄則」
良品計画前会長
松井忠三

[ジャパン・ブランドの挑戦01]

56 リラクゼーションを
新たなジャパン・ブランドに！
りらく　取締役会長　竹之内教博
代表取締役社長兼CEO　出上幸典

[ジャパン・ブランドの挑戦02]

86 伝統とノウハウをブランド化して、
日本の魚食文化を守りたい
ヤマセ村清　代表取締役社長　山崎祐嗣

[ジャパン・ブランドの挑戦03]

118 教習所がディズニーランドを超える日
武蔵境自動車教習所　代表取締役会長　髙橋　勇

[ジャパン・ブランドの挑戦04]

150 待ちのEMSから、
　　攻めのブランディングカンパニーへ
YURIホールディングス代表取締役、
エーピーアイ代表取締役　須田哲生

[ジャパン・ブランドの挑戦05]

180 ブランドが人材を呼び、
　　人材がブランドを高めていく好循環
関家具　専務　関 正

[未来へ続く]

210 企業ブランディングが切り開く、
　　ジャパン・ブランドの未来
イマジナ　代表取締役社長　関野吉記

Contents

08 Preface

[Special Interview]

16 The "Cardinal Rules" of a Globally Competitive Japan Brand
Tadamitsu Matsui
Former Chairman,
Ryohin Keikaku Co., Ltd.

[The Ascent of The Japan Brand 01]

56 **Making Relaxation into a New Japan Brand!**
Yukihiro Takenouchi, Chairman, riraku Co., LTD.
Yukinori Ideue, President and CEO, riraku Co., LTD.

[The Ascent of The Japan Brand 02]

86 **Branding Tradition And Know-How to Conserve The Fish Cuisine Culture of Japan**
Yuji Yamazaki, President, YAMASE MURASEI Co., LTD.

[The Ascent of the Japan Brand 03]

118 **The Day A Driving School Surpasses Disneyland**
Isamu Takahashi
Chairman, Musashisakai Driving School Co., LTD.

[The Ascent of The Japan Brand 04]

150 From Passive Electronics Manufacturing Services to a Proactive Branding Company

Tetsuo Suda
CEO, YURI Holdings, API Co.,Ltd.

[The Ascent of The Japan Brand 05]

180 A 'Virtuous Cycle' That Pulls in Talented Workers Who Elevate the Brand

Tadashi Seki
Executive Director, SEKI FURNITURE Co., Ltd.

[To Be Continued]

210 Corporate Branding to Cut a Path for the Future of Japan Brands

Yoshiki Sekino
President and CEO, imajina,inc.

はじめに

　私たちイマジナが、アメリカを中心に海外での成功を目指す日本企業のサポートを始めてから、早くも20年が経ちます。当初は、日本企業だけでなく、私たち自身も苦労の連続でした。

　日本企業は、ビジネス拠点や商品のグローバル化は大の得意でしたが、人材マネジメントの異文化対応が決定的に不得手でした。赴任者の研修はせいぜい語学の習得が中心で、現地に深く溶け込めず、無理に日本独自のやり方、考え方を押し通して摩擦やトラブルを生んでしまいます。そこから無数のネガティブなエピソードが生み出されて本国にフィードバックされ、かえって日本企業の「内弁慶さ」を誘発し、海外進出を思いとどまらせてしまうのです。

　ところが、この1、2年、変化が見え始めています。まず、日本企業の意識が変わってきました。大手企業は採用段階からグローバル展開を意識し始めました。中小企業、地方企業、そしてベンチャーでも、現状を打ち破り、果敢に海外に打って出ようという風潮が強くなっています。時代も大きく変わり始めています。TPP時代到来を控え、一段と競争が激しさを増す中で、少子高齢化と人口減少を迎える国内市場にこのまま固執していても成長が見込めないという覚悟が強まりました。そして、見逃せないのは、日本企業、つまり日本人自身による自己評価の変化です。成熟した国内市場の中で生き抜いてきた企業には、実はグローバルの舞台で思いもよらぬ強みを発揮できる力があるのではないかという自信の芽が生まれつつあります。やり方によっては、リスク回避どころではない、大きな成長をつかめるチャンスが訪れるかもしれないのです。

　日本人自ら「ガラパゴス」と揶揄することの多い日本の独自性が、一方で

Preface

20 years have passed since we at imajina inc. begun providing support to Japanese companies aiming to succeed overseas, mainly in America. At the outset, it was not just the companies we supported which were struggling: we also had a hard time.

Japanese companies, while remarkably adept at taking their business hubs and commercial products to the global audience, showed decidedly little aptitude for dealing with aspects related to human resource management in different cultures. Employees dispatched abroad only received training in the form of some language classes, could not manage to assimilate into local areas, and thus ended up causing trouble and discord by dogmatically attempting to foist their Japanese approach and philosophy onto local personnel. This led to several negative episodes, which were fed back to Japan, provoking the idea that Japanese companies were only "tough on their own turf," and calling the idea of advancing overseas into question.

Having said that, in the last year or two, change is becoming apparent. Firstly, Japanese companies have undergone a shift in awareness. Major corporations have started to approach global expansion even from the employment stage. There is a palpable mood shift - among SMEs, local companies and venture companies - toward breaking out of the current rut and intrepidly striking out overseas. The era is also starting to change quite significantly. With the onset of the TPP era in which competition will become increasingly fierce, there is growing realization that growth cannot be expected despite persistence and tenacity in the domestic market that is dogged by a falling birth rate and an aging and shrinking population. One more crucial element to consider is that Japanese companies, in other words Japanese people themselves, are undergoing a change in how they rate themselves. Companies who managed to thrive in a mature domestic market are starting

はモノやサービスの質の高さ、ホスピタリティ、独自の歴史・伝統とその背景にある文化といった形で、ポジティブな評価を浴び始めています。「ジャパン・ブランド」、つまり海外から評価されるブランドとしての日本が、確実に存在感を増しています。その果実を享受したければ、私たちは世界の多様性の大きな一角を担う日本人として、自信を持って海外に打って出ればいいのです。

アンテナを高く張っている企業ほど、いち早くその価値に気づき始めています。とても喜ばしいことですし、長年の苦労を考えるとき、ついにここまで来たかと感無量です。

「ジャパン・ブランド」を引っさげてグローバル市場で勝負する以上は、「ジャパン・ブランド」を評価する側の視点に立たなければならないのは自明です。放っておいても優秀な社員が辞めない、何も言わなくてもまじめに力を出してくれる風土は、日本だけが持っている極めて特殊な文化的、社会的状況であり、国籍も人種も文化も宗教も違う、ダイバーシティにあふれた海外では、それでは誰も察してくれません。それどころか、優秀な人材をつなぎ止められず、ステークホルダーをまとめられないのです。

外側だけでなく、内側に向けてのブランド構築も、これからは必須です。では、どうすれば自分たちの力を結集し、グローバルの舞台で問えるのでしょうか？

その答えこそが、自らのブランドの構築です。言うまでもなく、築き上げた自社のブランドは、「ジャパン・ブランド」と直結します。

本書は、まさに今、ブランドを構築して自らの殻を破ろうとしているさまざまな企業の姿をお伝えします。そして、私たちイマジナが考える企業ブランディングと「ジャパン・ブランド」の未来を提示していきます。巻頭に、「ジャパン・ブランド」の先駆者として成長を続ける「無印良品」を指揮した良品計画の松

to show "green shoots" of confidence in the fact that they are actually very well poised to draw on their strengths on the global stage. Depending on the approach, rather than merely averting risk, it is possible to get important opportunities conducive to growth.

Japanese people tend to be mocked for their idiosyncratic "Galapagos" syndrome; yet on another front, more and more there is a great deal of positivity about Japan for the high quality of its services and products, hospitality, unique history and traditions and the underlying culture. The "Japan Brand," in other words Japan itself as a brand, is starting to be recognized overseas. If we wish to reap the fruits of this, we as Japanese must be unrestrained in casting our nets overseas as people comprising one great slice of the world's diversity.

The higher a company has raised its antenna, the sooner it will discover this value. It is a most pleasing fact and when I recall the many years of hard work, I am full of emotion to realize how long the journey has been for Japanese companies.

Winning in the global market by striking with the "Japan Brand" relies upon putting yourself in the shoes of the people on the other side who are evaluating it; this fact speaks for itself. The endemic culture in Japan - whereby talented employees will not quit even if left alone and where people earnestly do their best without being asked to - is an extremely particular cultural and societal set of conditions unique to Japan. In other countries that are richly diverse in terms of nationalities, races, cultures and religions, nobody will observe this cultural climate. Worse still, talented employees will leave the company and problems with stakeholders may ensue as a result.

What will also become important in the coming months and years will be constructing inward-oriented brand construction, not just outward. In which case, how exactly should companies go about concentrating their capabilities to emerge onto the global stage?

はじめに

井忠三前会長をお迎えできたのは喜びの至りであるとともに、これからチャレンジしていく人たちを大いに勇気づけていただけるはずです。

　本書独自の取り組みとして、今回、すべての文章に英語による対訳を掲載しました。これは、日本流のクオリティコントロールの秘密、企業の安定性、そして「ジャパン・ブランド」の源泉と舞台裏を全世界に発信していきたいという、私たちの夢、あるいは「野心」です。日本の価値観と世界の標準が互いに出合い、クロスオーバーしている。それこそが、今の時代の雰囲気だと思うのです。

　これまでの「学歴」や「家柄」の時代は終わり、「魂」の時代、つまり「人柄」がすべてを決める時代が来ました。いいか悪いかはさておき、各人の二極化、つまりリッチな人とそうではない人の切り分けは避けられません。変化を受け入れる者が生き残り、変化できない者は消えていく。企業もまた同じです。今まで生き抜いてきたからといって、そのまま変化せずにいると、あっという間に陳腐化します。今日やらなければ明日退場せざるを得なくなるかもしれない時代です。しかし、私たちには幸いにも、生まれ持って身についている「ジャパン・ブランド」があります。しかもその評価は年々高まっています。最初は怖いかもしれませんが、実は日本人、日本企業というだけで、高いブランド価値を持つものとしてポジティブに受け止めてもらえるのです。生まれたばかりの企業でも、何代にもわたって事業と想いを受け継いできたブランドでも、大会社でも中小企業でも関係ありません。実はすべてが強みなのです。だからこそ、日本で大切にしてきたモノを、想いを、ブランドとして構築し直そうではありませんか。

　私たちイマジナは、想いをもう一度見つめ直してブランドを構築し、世界に

Preface

This very answer lies in establishing ones own brand. Needless to say, a well-developed "own company" brand directly connects to the "Japan Brand."

This book showcases various companies who are at this very moment attempting to construct their own brands and shed their old skin. It will also introduce imajina's approach to corporate branding and the future of the "Japan Brand". It is with our utmost joy that the book opens with a chapter featuring RYOHIN KEIKAKU CO., LTD.'s honorary adviser Mr.Tadamitsu Matsui –the man who pioneered the "Japan Brand" and led the ever-succesful MUJI – and who will surely inspire confidence in anyone thinking of taking up the challenge.

As a unique feature, this book includes a parallel English translation. This springs from a dream of ours, an "ambition" to transmit to the world the secrets behind Japanese quality control, corporate stability as well as giving a glimpse of the essence and the back end of the "Japan Brand." The Japanese sense of values and global standards are beginning to intersect. I think that is exactly what the mood of the current era is.

The era of "academic record" and "family lineage" is over, replaced by an era where everything is contingent upon ones "soul" or "personal character." Irrespective of whether it is a good or bad thing, we cannot avoid the polarization of people, in other words, a carving into two groups of people who are spiritually rich and people who are not. Those who are open to change will survive, and those who fail to adopt will fade away. It is the same for companies. The minute you start to believe that because you have made it up until now you can just carry on without the need to evolve, you will be confined to obsolesce. This is an era where failing to act today could mean having to bow out tomorrow. However, fortunately for us, we were born with an innate sense of the "Japan Brand." What is more, this is increasingly well received year after year. While somewhat uncanny, the fact is that people and companies are positively accepted as being of high brand value just by nature of being Japanese. It makes no difference if it is a fledgling company,

はじめに

打って出るお手伝いをしています。ブランドが明確になれば、顧客だけでなく、人材もどんどん引き寄せられます。従業員の力を引き出せます。業績が伸びていく姿が嬉しくなり、仕事が楽しくてたまらなくなります。すると、働く人の表情が変わり、月曜日に会社に行くのが楽しくなります。本当はそんな企業で、誰もが働きたいはずです。そして、硬直感のない、のびのびとした働き方が実現できる社会こそ、日本企業が世界から学ばなければならないグローバル・スタンダードです。私たちは、その一助となりたいのです。

本書は、自らの課題を認識し、ブランド構築と成長へのチャレンジを続けているさまざまな企業にインタビューし、まさに今の取り組みの現状や想いを率直に語っていただきました。読者の皆さんには、その行間に、未来を切り拓こうとしているスピリットと情熱を感じ、変革へのヒントと勇気を見出していただければ幸いです。

日本、日本人、そして日本企業の飛躍は、まさにこれから始まるのです。

2015年　12月
株式会社イマジナ　代表取締役　奥山由実子

Preface

a brand that has been passed down with a business and philosophy for many generations, whether it is a big corporation or an SME. In fact, everything is to their advantage. For this very reason, it is time for Japanese people and Japanese companies to reconstruct the products and philosophies long cherished in Japan, as brands.

At imajina, we are in the business of supporting companies to take a fresh look at their philosophies in order to construct their brands and take on the global competition. If the brand is definitively constructed, it will attract customers but also pull in talented staff. It will draw out the abilities of employees. Delighted at the sight of healthily growing results, work becomes genuinely enjoyable. Employees display a new expression on their faces, and look forward to going to work on a Monday morning. Anybody would want to work at such a company as this. On top of this, Japanese companies must learn the global standard from around the world pursuant to a society that is not overly rigid and where work can be fulfilling. We want to be contributory to this.

This book was made possible through interviews with various companies who are aware of their respective challenges, and who are committed to working toward brand building and growth. They were candid in sharing their current states of mind and initiatives. I hope that readers can read between the lines to get a sense of the spirit and passion that is pioneering the future, as well as discovering inspiration for innovation, and true courage.

The ascent of Japan, Japanese people and Japanese companies has only just begun.

Yumiko Okuyama, Representative Director, imajina, inc.
December 2015

特別インタビュー

世界を勝ちジャパン・「鉄則」

良品計画前会長
松井忠三

抜いていくブランドの

**ジャパン・ブランドの旗手
「MUJI」を率いた松井忠三が語る、
正しいブランドの作り方**

12期連続増収、4期連続増益。
ニューヨークで、パリで、ロンドンで、そしてアジアで。
海外300店舗の「MUJI」が、成長とブランドを支えている。
日本発のブランドが、どのように構築されたのか。
そのリアルなストーリーとノウハウを、社長・会長を7年ずつ務め、
2015年、後進に道を譲った松井忠三氏に聞いた。文中、敬称略

| 特別インタビュー | 良品計画前会長 | 松井忠三 |

ブランドには思想と戦略がある

　無印良品は、自らをブランドとは定義していない。しかし、私たちが無印良品から感じ取るメッセージは、ブランドそのものだ。松井が無印良品の最大の強みとしてまず指摘したのは、無印良品が当初からコンセプト、哲学に立脚していたことだった。無印良品は、単にシリーズ化された商品群ではなく、ライフスタイルそのものを提案、販売している生活雑貨専門店であるということ。つまり、ライバルはIKEAしかいない。そしてもうひとつは、立ち上げの当初から、一貫してSPA（製造小売業）であることだという。

　初の海外進出が1991年で、しかも1号店がロンドンだったという事実にも驚かされる。当時、ジャパン・ブランドなどという言葉は、まだどこにもなかったに違いない。しかし、先駆者としての無印良品が今日に至るまでの道のりは、決して単純な右肩上がりではなく、むしろ紆余曲折を経ている。そこにこそ、現在の無印良品が持っている、本当のブランドの強さが隠れている。

　1980年代初頭、日本の低成長時代の幕が開いた時、総合スーパー（GMS）は競ってプライベートブランド（PB）商品を開発、展開した。無印良品も、1980年、西友のPBとして、40アイテムでスタートした。当時PBは、「ノーブランド」と呼ばれた。

　同時期に始まったPBで、現在まで続いているものは他にない。その上、アイテム数は7000まで拡大しているのだという。もはや、無印良品をノーブランドと呼ぶ人はいないだろう。PBは、次第に経営が苦しくなるGMSが、価格競争力を強めるためにコストを削減する手段だった。しかし、無印良品だけが抱えているものがあった。松井は言う。

「唯一、無印だけが、最初から思想と戦略を持っていたのです」

天才マーケッターのミニマリズム

　PBでありながら、立ち上げの当初からブランドだった無印良品。そのコンセプトを作ったのは、セゾングループ（当時は西武流通グループ）の総帥、故堤清二だった。

　PBは、基本的に経済合理性の権化である。ナショナルブランドよりも安くて、品質的に納得できる商品を、極限までローコストで供給すること。まさに、低成長かつ成熟した時代の申し子だった。だが、顧客はPB商品を「安かろう悪かろう」の典型とみなすようになり、次第に飽き始める。その中で、無印良品だけが、顧客になぜ自分たちの商品が安いのかを説明することに努めていた。「百貨店のクオリティを7割の価格で販売する」理由を、合理性だけでなく、「消費社会へのアンチテーゼ」として訴えた。

　見栄えだけのために、本来食べられるはずの食材を切り捨てないようにする。品質に問題のない限り、容器は共通のモノを使う。衣料品からは、糊付け、アイロン掛けだけでなくパッケージさえもなくしてしまう。「わけあって安い」のだ。そして、追求した結果のシンプルさ、簡潔さを、個性として昇華させ、前に押し出していく。ただコストを削り、包装を簡略化し、安さだけで顧客を惹きつけようとするのではなかった。PBでありながらデザインのコストは削減せず、当時日本のグラフィックデザインをリードしていた故田中一光に依頼して、今日にまで続くデザインを生み出した。禅や茶道の価値観にも通じる、日本の文化に原点を持つ本質的なミニマリズムの提案。それが、作家、詩人としても知られる天才的マーケッター・堤清二が描いた、無印良品の本質だった。

　1983年、それまでは西友の店舗内だけで展開していた無印良品は、初めて東京・青山に単独の直営路面店舗を出店する。当時西友の社員だった松

井は、あまりの好況ぶりに驚いた。

「年間の予算を1ヵ月で達成するような、大盛況でした」

ビジネスとしての手応えを確実にした無印良品は、1989年に西友から独立し、いきなり海外に進出することになる。

1991年、ロンドンに海外1号店を出店

無印良品のコンセプトを作った堤清二は、セゾングループの旗艦でありながら、百貨店としては後発だった西武百貨店を一流に押し上げるため、欧米に人材を送り、西武でしか入手できない海外ブランドの開拓に腐心していた。

西武百貨店のビジネスパートナーだったロンドンの老舗百貨店、リバティの担当者の眼に、無印良品のコンセプトが留まった。これならヨーロッパでも十分に通用する確信があるという。こうして、世界中のブランドを「輸入」していた西武が、今度は反対にヨーロッパから「輸出」しないかと誘われることになった。堤清二の心にも、海外で通用しないブランドは決して日本で生き残れないという思いがあったという。

無印良品のスタートから10年あまり、良品計画として独立してからわずか2年で、ロンドンのど真ん中に店を出すことになった。このスピード感は、カリスマと呼ばれた堤清二だからこそ、そしてバブル景気のピーク時の日本だからこそ可能なチャレンジだったのかもしれない。

「内側から見ていても、驚くべきスピード感でしたよ」

1991年に西友から良品計画に出向し、人事や給与計算の制度構築を最前線で担っていた松井の眼にさえ、セゾングループの当時の勢いは目を瞠るものがあったという。

ロンドン、ウエストエンド。木造3階建ての風格あるリバティ百貨店別館の一角に、無印良品の海外1号店がオープンした。田中一光をはじめとするデザイナー陣をロンドンに送り込み、妥協なく店舗を作り込んだ。当初は、味噌や醤油など食材まで扱っていたが、食文化の違いから苦戦し、次第に衣料品と生活雑貨に特化していく。同年、ロンドンに次いで香港にアジア1号店をオープン。その後、シンガポールにも展開していくことになった。
　こうして、現在300店舗にも上る「MUJI」の海外展開の第一歩が刻まれた。

セゾンの栄光と挫折

　MUJIは、イギリスの先進的なデザイナーをはじめ、教養のある層や先見性の高い層に好意的に迎えられた。彼らはMUJIの中に日本を感じながら、自分たちの生活に取り入れていった。アジアでも、熱狂的とでも言うべき歓迎ぶりだったという。しかし、海外展開7年目、1997年のMUJI店舗数は、ヨーロッパ5、アジア7の計12店舗に過ぎなかった。
「一般の消費者には、なかなか浸透しなかった」
　松井がそう振り返る1990年代の後半、追い打ちをかけるようにアジア通貨危機が起こり、1998年にはアジアから全面撤退することになる。ヨーロッパでも、消費の枠組みが変調し始めていた。
「日本と同様、百貨店というビジネスモデルが崩れてしまった」
　成熟期を迎えた先進国のマーケットでは、消費者がそれぞれの個性に応じてモノを選び始めるようになる。すると、価格が高くても1ヵ所ですべてまかなえ、しかもその店の敷居をまたぐことそのものにブランド価値を見出せる百貨店よりも、自己の価値観だけを追求し、より細かなニーズを満たせ、価格面ではシビア

な要求に応えてくれる専門店が好まれるようになるのだ。こうして、カテゴリーキラーの専門店が登場するたび、百貨店は苦戦を強いられることになる。リバティ百貨店も、業績が振るわず経営者が変わり、MUJIと袂を分かつことになった。

そもそも、イギリス独特の契約条件が重くのしかかり、MUJIは赤字経営が続いていた。それでも本国日本での経営が順調な間は、無印良品のブランド価値への投資として支えることが正当化された。しかし、セゾングループはバブル崩壊の過程で多額の負債を抱え、リストラと資産売却の嵐に襲われていた。

2001年、セゾングループは事実上解体。グループ内では優良企業だった良品計画も、海外撤退などの損失がかさみ、同年中間期に38億円の赤字を計上する。

「必ずしも、ずっと順調に進んできたわけではないのです」

松井が社長に就任したのが、まさに2001年だった。

「勝つ構造」の再構築

立て直しに当たって松井は、当時のトップアナリストから、こんな厳しい言葉を聞かされたという。

「『一度凋落した専門店が、復活することはない』というのです。確かに、過去の例を思い起こせばその通りで、対症療法はできても、根治に成功した例は、私にも浮かばなかった」

赤字なら、ひとまずリストラすればよい。経費を圧縮し、人件費を削減し、赤字店舗を閉鎖する。しかし、それで本当に無印良品の良さを再び消費者に訴える「勝つ構造」を再構築することができるのだろうか? 松井は自問し続けた。

「私は、無印良品を生み出した『セゾンの文化』こそが、実は足かせだった

のではないかと思い至ったのです」

　西武百貨店を一流に育て、無印良品だけでなく、パルコやファミリーマートなど時代を先読みした業態を次々に創出したセゾン。だが、科学的なオペレーションを追求する力は、決定的に弱かった。

「百貨店は『個店主義』です。個々の店の魅力が際立っていることが大切で、改装や増床を先手を打って行い、常に発信力を高める必要があります。チェーンオペレーションとは、正反対なのです」

　そして、その中心にいたのは、言うまでもなく天才マーケッター、堤清二その人だった。天才はひとりいればいい。周囲は背中を見て、意を汲み、現場の意見を主張せず、暗黙知で仕事をつないでいく。それがセゾングループに深く根付いていた独特のやり方だった。右肩上がりの時期で、天才がいるうちはそれでいい。しかし、個人主義、経験主義が行き過ぎれば、その人がいなくなった時点でブランドの核が消えてしまうことになる。同様に、ある店舗から優秀な店長がいなくなれば、やがてその店自体が立ち行かなくなる。また、店長がだめなら、そもそも周囲は成長のしようもない。

　一時代を築いたセゾンの文化は、近代小売業の商業理論からは、およそ離れたところに来てしまっていたのだ。

一流の戦略よりも、一流の実行力

　松井の改革の第一歩は、初めからハードだった。

「専務と社長では、体感的には責任が20倍くらい違います」

　今でこそ、松井の表情には笑顔が浮かぶ。リストラを断行し、売価ベースで100億円もの不良在庫を処分した。フランスの店舗も閉鎖した。が、松井

が本当に踏み込むべきと考えたのは、表面的な数字では表せない、いわばカルチャーのようなものだった。松井は、良品計画の社内に蔓延していた「大企業病」の根治に努めたのである。

　無印良品が名の通ったブランドになった結果、前例踏襲、事なかれ主義がはびこるようになっていた。カリスマ経営者の率いるトップダウン型の組織だから、どうせ下から主張しても通らない。出る杭は打たれるから黙る。社員同士で責任をなすりつけ合う……。

　松井は、こうしたセゾン独特の文化を変え、社内の雰囲気を一掃しなければ、どれだけ無印良品のブランドが確立されていようと、決して生き残れないと確信した。変化の速さについていけず、遠からず、モノを作る力も発信力も弱くなっていくからだ。

「戦略が一流で、実行力が二流の会社と、戦略は二流でも実行力は一流の会社があるとします。生き残るのは必ず後者です。セゾンの常識は、世間の非常識だったのです」

　松井は、無印良品が20年以上抱えてきた企業文化を、根底から変え始めた。社員一人ひとりの中に実行力と責任を持たせ、全社的な足腰を強化する。そのために、すべての業務を「仕組み化」し、マニュアルを整備して「見える化」する。こうして、劇的な業績回復の原動力となった合計2000ページにも及ぶマニュアル「MUJIGRAM（ムジグラム）」の策定が始まった。

ブランドは戦略だけでは成立しない

　「MUJIGRAM」には、店舗での売り場作りや接客はもとより、顧客の声をどのように汲み上げるのか、追加発注はどんなフラグによってどう判断するのか、

それを受けて増産や減産をいつ決断するのか、誰が見ても納得でき、理解して取り組める内容を盛り込んだ。これによって、教育・研修の均一化や責任の明確化が図られた。各店舗が均質化でき、すべきことに全社一斉に取り組めるようになった。

　責任の所在もはっきりわかるようになった。無印良品のイメージだけでビジネスを押し通すのではなく、コンセプトを大切にしながらも、それを業績に変える実行力を併せ持った企業風土が作られていった。
「ブランドは、すばらしい戦略やコンセプトがあっても、実行力がなければ何にもならないのです」

　ゼロは何度掛け合わせても、ゼロにしかならない。カリスマの遺したコンセプトを大切にしながら、それを実行していく力を鍛える。それこそが、無印良品のブランドを持続させ、強化する礎となった。

　2002年には再び黒字化。2015年2月期まで12年連続の増収を続け、まもなく営業利益は300億円を超える水準に達する見通しだという。中でも、海外での売上高が、2015年2月期で約770億円、2016年2月期は1000億円をうかがう勢いというのも驚かされる。1990年代末、一度ゼロになったアジアの店舗数は、2015年10月時点で255。今や、大きく利益に貢献している。
「しかし、海外展開もまた、苦難の歴史でした」

　そう語る松井には、海外店舗の再構築も、明確な考え方があった。そこに、MUJIがジャパン・ブランドになっていく過程が隠されていた。

無理に背伸びをしても、ブランドは育たない

　松井は、海外、とりわけ欧米におけるMUJIブランドの確立が、日本国内や

アジア市場での成長の原動力になっていることを否定はしない。ただ、松井はこう断言する。

「異文化にブランドを受容してもらうには、たとえいいモノであろうと長い時間がかかる。その間、ビジネスとしてサステナブルでなければならないのです」

ブランドイメージの箔付けのためだけに、やみくもに欧米に進出して赤字の山を築いてしまえば、かえってブランド価値を毀損してしまう、ということなのだ。松井のこの信念は、苦い記憶に根ざしている。

アジアから撤退し、リバティ百貨店との提携を解消した後、無印良品の海外展開は、100％自社のビジネスとして再スタートすることになった。1998年当時は、ヨーロッパに10店舗を展開している状況だった。だが、セゾングループの存亡をかけた瀬戸際の攻防の中で、優良企業だった無印良品の株価を、どうしても高いまま維持したいというグループ内での思惑があった。海外展開の進展は、日本におけるブランド価値の上昇、そして投資家のイメージを向上させ、株価を高止まりさせる支援材料になる。そのような判断から、比較的うまく展開できていたフランスを中心に、店舗数を大幅に増やすことになった。松井が社長に就任した2001年時点では、倍増以上の21店舗。しかもその大半は赤字だった。

「海外での攻めが難しいことは、当時でもよくわかっていました。しかし、そのまま進めてしまった。もちろん、そのおかげで短期的にMUJIのブランド価値は向上したかもしれませんが、やがて限界が来ます」

リスクでしかない、質を伴わない成長

背伸びをしても、決してブランドは育たない。それがわかっていながら、お家

Special Interview | Ryohin Keikaku Former Chairman | Tadamitsu Matsui

の事情で出店を続けてしまった。松井が社長に就任した後、海外の店舗もリストラの対象になったことはいうまでもない。しかしMUJIは、スピードこそ緩やかではあれ、それなりに欧州で受容されてきた。なぜ赤字店舗ばかりなのか、社長になった松井はさっそく分析にとりかかった。

ロンドン繁華街にある店舗は、決して悪くない売上を計上していた。ただ、地価の高いロンドンとはいえ、家賃があまりに高すぎた。人件費や物流経費は、たとえ海外でも、ある程度自主的にコントロールできる。一方で家賃は長期に渡る契約で、後から高いと気づいても解約できない。焦って出店を急いだ結果、物件を費用対効果の面から吟味する余裕がなく、身の丈に合った、サステナブルな店舗運営ができていなかったのだ。

コアなMUJIファンがいて、ある程度のリピーターが確保できていても、これではいつまでも黒字化できない。まして、成熟したヨーロッパ市場では、ブランドの浸透に時間がかかる。長期戦に対応できる出店展開でなければ、ビジネスとして持続できない。

「質を伴わない成長は、リスクでしかない」松井はそう言い切った。

可能であれば、すべての店舗が黒字であるべき。それが厳しくとも、宣伝目的での展開と割り切って業績の足を引っ張るようなことは認めない。そのためには、いたずらに規模だけを拡大するのではなく、1店舗ベースで、しかも現地の本社機能の運営経費も併せて軌道に乗ってから、じっくり次の店舗展開、そして新しい国への進出を考える。こうした考えのもと、赤字店舗を損失覚悟で閉鎖しながら、より経済的な物件に新たな店舗を設けた。

不採算店から撤退しつつ、ゆっくり店舗数、進出国は増えていった。英仏独に次いで、イタリア、アメリカ、カナダ、オーストラリアに展開。欧米で73店舗を数えるまでに成長した。そしてこの苦労が、比類なきブランドとしてアジ

アでの大成功に貢献する。

無二のジャパン・ブランドはこうして作られた

　欧米で苦難の10年間を過ごす一方、いったん完全撤退したアジアには、松井が社長に就任した2001年から再進出を果たした。それからわずか15年で255店舗を数えるまでに急成長し、収益に貢献できる大きな柱に育った。MUJIが無二のジャパン・ブランドになれた理由は、どこにあったのだろうか。松井が理由として挙げた無印良品の最大の強みを、もう一度思い出してみよう。

　無印良品は、当初からコンセプト、哲学に立脚していて、ライフスタイルを売る業態だったこと。そして、一貫してSPAであったことだ。松井は、MUJIブランドがグローバルにおいて成立する条件を、次のように説明した。

グローバル化を成立させる条件

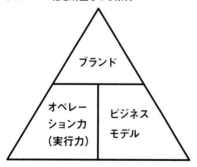

　まず、無印良品はブランドを頂点に置き、しっかりとした日本発の哲学を感じてもらえた上で、ライフスタイルを販売する。そして、ブランドを支える土台が、実行力とビジネスモデルだ。実行力を支えるのがMUJIGRAM。そしてビジネ

スモデルがSPAであることなのだ。

「販売する私たち自身が、顧客の特色をよく理解しながらモノ作りを進められる。すると、成功率も利益率も高まるのです」

　SPAだからこそ、ブランドの純度が高まっていく。ブランドが浸透すれば、利益率が上がっていく。それが松井の見出した成功哲学だった。

欧米とアジアでは
MUJIに対するイメージが大きく異なる！

　MUJIは日本発のブランドではあるが、その受容度は一様ではない。海外進出を再構築しながら得た感覚を、松井はこんな言葉で表現した。

「ヨーロッパは『こだま』。でもアジアでは『のぞみ』になる」

　真っ先にMUJIのコンセプトを受け入れてくれたヨーロッパだが、個々人では熱心に支持してくれる人がいる反面、その数は少数派である。成長が止まり、中間層の生活が厳しくなりつつあるマーケットでは、日本人が考える以上にハイブランドの経営は苦しい。それ自体は単価の低いMUJIには向いているが、浸透はどうしても「各駅停車」なのだ。

　顧客に丁寧に説明し、ブランドの背景を説明していく。そのおかげで、ヨーロッパでは利益を出しにくい状況ではありながら、MUJIのブランド感は日本よりもむしろ高くすることができた。それを補ったのが、若い中間層が爆発的に増えているアジア、とりわけ中国市場だった。

　成熟したヨーロッパとは違い、収入が伸びて、もっと良いモノが買える生活に胸を躍らせている若い人が大勢いる。オリジナルのブランドを築くことは難しいが、すでに先進国で成功したブランドは、クオリティの高さ、洗練度、そし

| 特別インタビュー | 良品計画前会長 | 松井忠三 |

て安心感をもって評価される。さらに浸透のスピードも「特急」なのだ。

　松井は、中国では複数の地元企業と提携しながら、大胆な出店を続けた。今や、ユニクロやZARA、H&M、そして香港のドラッグストアチェーン・ワトソンズとともに、中国の「勝ち組」ショッピングモールに欠かせないテナントとなった。アジアでのMUJIは、完全に高級品の部類と受け入れられる。日本で生まれ、ヨーロッパで洗練されたブランド。生活の質を上げ、環境を考える哲学を持っている。そんなイメージが、すでに確立されている。

海外にどうやってMUJIの思いを伝えるのか?

「基本的に、欧米では宣伝をしません」

　日本では廉価かつ機能的なイメージのある無印良品だが、欧米ではブランドとしてとらえられている。それはブランドイメージの向上だけでなく、MUJIのコンセプトを好む顧客層の購買力の高さ、そして輸送コストの上乗せが必要となる供給側の現実的な問題もあいまって起きている現象だ。つまり、深い部分でのコンセプトへの理解と共感がなければ、軽々しく手を出せるものではない。

　新規店舗を展開する際は、MUJIのブランドが理解できるポスターを貼り、印刷物を用意する。文化的な背景、MUJIの歴史、モノ作りへのこだわり。なぜこの値段で、こうしたライフスタイルを提供するのかを語りかけ、ただ商品を気に入ってもらうのではなく、コンセプトを好きになってもらうこと。パリでもミラノでもデュッセルドルフでも、地道でありながら正面から努力を続けてきたという。

　松井が強く戒めていることがある。まず、純広告をぶつけないこと。異文化において、MUJIのコンセプトは純広告では伝わらないと判断しているのだ。そこにコストをかけるくらいなら、むしろ価格を下げるべきだと考える。代わりにメ

ディア関係者を招待し、丁寧な説明をする機会を作ることにした。もうひとつは、ジャパン・ブランドで勝負しながら、決して現地在住の日本人や日本人観光客を頼らないこと。

　もちろん、日本人お断りというのではない。ただ、その国で暮らす人に直接響かなければ、絶対に事業として持続できない。グローバル化が進めば進むほど、モノもカネも国境を軽く飛び越え、良いモノをわざわざ買いに来る動機は減っていくからだ。細かく国民性や文化の違うヨーロッパで、そこに暮らす人を相手にビジネスを続けること。それがブランドとしてのMUJIを根付かせると同時に、アジア各国での圧倒的な高級感の構築につながっているのだ。

現地従業員のインナーブランディング

　一方で、海外のMUJI店舗の最前線で実行力を支えるのは、あくまで現地採用の従業員である。彼らもMUJIのブランドを支えている重要な登場人物だ。

　日本では、MUJIGRAMでしっかりと仕組み化し、モノ作り、販売、経営、人材育成のすべてを標準化できたが、欧米では独特の難しさがあるという。

　当初は、商品企画の機能までヨーロッパに置き、現地のニーズに合うアイテムを供給していた。しかし、仕組みが浸透していないためにクオリティコントロールが難しく、大切にしなければならないはずのMUJIのコンセプトから離れたアイテムが店頭に並ぶようになってしまったことがある。

「ヨーロッパは歴史がある分、従業員も自分たちで進めようとする気概を持っている。ただ、そこに仕組みを持ち込まなければ、やがてかつてのセゾンのようになってしまう危険性があります」

　松井は今後のヨーロッパ事業の課題をこう分析する。むしろ北米のほうが、

仕組み化の受け入れに関してはスムーズに進むという。一方で、中国ではすでに1200ページ相当のローカライズ版MUJIGRAMが作成されている。毎年30店舗以上を出店し、700〜800人の新たな従業員が加わるというから、現地の制度を取り入れながらも、仕事を見える化し、仕組み化で実行力を担保することが大切になる。中身も頻繁にアップデートされる。中国が日本と違うのは、完全な個人主義の社会だということだ。当然、商習慣も異なるし、店長とスタッフが一致団結して難題に当たるような組織は期待しにくい。しかし、中国の消費者がMUJIに期待するのは、あくまで日本のようなクオリティだ。そこで店舗単位ではなく、個人単位でMUJIGRAMの改良提案をした社員を表彰するようにし、経営から人材育成までを、中国流でありながらジャパン・ブランドを保つように整えた。MUJIの挑戦と拡大は、こうして続いていく。

ジャパン・ブランドが勝ち抜いていく方法

ジャパン・ブランドの旗手として、地に足の着いたビジネスを展開してきた松井。今後のジャパン・ブランドの展望と、後に続くであろう人たちへのアドバイスを聞いてみた。
「ジャパン・ブランドの評価は二極化しています」
ユニクロやダイソー、TOTOの衛生陶器やダイキンのエアコン。あるいは味千ラーメンは、海外でより強いブランドを築いている。しかし、日本の家電メーカーのブランド価値は、みるみる減少してしまった。どこに差があるのだろうか。
「その地域に根ざした、ローカライゼーションを受け入れられるかどうか。ここが最大のポイントだと思います」
日本のブランドをそのまま持って行くだけでは勝てない。日本では圧倒的な某

大手うどんチェーンが中国市場で苦戦したのは、うどんのコシが原因だったという。コンセプトは残しつつローカライズできるかで、成功できるかどうかが分かれていく。無印良品のように中国やアジアで大成功しているのであれば、そこに特化すればいいのではないか、という疑問も湧く。だが、松井は明確にそれを否定した。

「比較的嗜好性の近いアジアにまずはチャレンジする、というのは現実的な経営判断でしょう。ただ、それでも欧米を勝ち抜いた強いブランドこそが、世界を席巻する力を持つと考えます」

低成長のヨーロッパにあって、シャネルやグッチのビジネスモデルはいまだに崩れてはいない。なぜなら、それまで培ったブランドを武器に、グローバルマーケットで勝負できているからだ。何もハイブランドには限らない。シビアなヨーロッパの中間層を相手に成長してきたZARAやIKEAも、やはりそこで獲得したブランドイメージを世界で展開し、成功している。松井は言う。

「迷っているくらいなら、思い切って早く海外に行くほうがいい、できることなら1店舗でいいから、先進国に出てみたほうがいい。どんなに調べ、外から研究しても、実際に出てみなければわからないシビアさが、山のようにあります。そこで黒字化できるかどうかが、世界的なブランドを構築する第一歩になるはずです」

今後のインド市場への進出が発表された。ジャパン・ブランドの先駆者として、MUJIのこれからに期待したい。

まつい・ただみつ
1949年静岡県生まれ。73年東京教育大学（現・筑波大学）体育学部卒業後、西友ストアー（現・西友）入社。92年良品計画へ。総務人事部長、無印良品事業部長を経て2001年社長に就任。08年から務めた会長を2015年5月21日に退任、名誉顧問に。

Special Interview

THE "CARDIN A GLOBALLY JAPAN BRAND

Former Chairman of Ryohin Keikaku Co., Ltd.
Tadamitsu Matsui

AL RULES" OF COMPETITIVE

The correct approach to brand building as described by Tadamitsu Matsui, the force behind MUJI becoming the quintessential Japan Brand.

Increased revenues for 12 consecutive periods, increased profits for four consecutive periods. In New York, in Paris, in London, and in Asia. With 300 overseas stores, MUJI bolsters its growth and its brand. How was this Japan-born brand formed? Mr. Tadamitsu Matsui served as president and chairman for seven years in each position, before making way for new blood in 2015. Here, he shares the real story and know-how behind the company's ascent.

Concept and Strategy Co-Exist Within the Brand

MUJI does not define itself in terms of being a brand. The message that we take in from MUJI, however, constitutes the very brand itself. The first thing that Matsui identified as MUJI's greatest strength was that from the outset, it was rooted in concept and philosophy. Rather than merely being a group of products released in a series, MUJI is a specialist general goods store that proposes real lifestyles. Put simply, its only peer is IKEA.

Another facet of MUJI is that since establishment, it has consistently remained a Specialty Store Retailer of Private Label Apparel (SPA). A truly astonishing feat was opening its first overseas store in London in 1991. This was a time long before expressions like "Japan Brand" entered the lexicon. The story so far for trailblazing MUJI, however, has not been one of steadily increasing growth; in fact, it has been full of trials and tribulations. Concealed within this turbulent trajectory is the true strength of the brand that MUJI possesses today.

When Japan's era of low growth began to unfold in the early 1980s, general merchandise stores (GMS) competitively developed and leveraged private brand (PB) products. In 1980, as a PB of The Seiyu Ltd., MUJI started out with around 40 items. At that juncture, the PB was called "no-brand."

There are no other private brands still going today that started in this same period. What is more, MUJI has expanded to offer 7,000 items. Suffice to say, no one refers to MUJI as "no-brand" any more. For PB, general merchandize stores took the step of cutting costs to bolster competitiveness. PB provided GMS - facing increasingly tough management conditions - with a tool to bolster cost competitiveness.

However, there was something that only MUJI had. Matsui explains:

"MUJI was alone in having both philosophy and strategy right from the start."

The Minimalism of a Genius Marketer

Despite being a private brand, MUJI was a brand in its own right from the outset. Behind this concept was Saison Group (at that time Seibu Distribution Group) leader The late Seiji Tsutsumi.

Private brands are basically the incarnation of economic rationality. The key is to supply items of reasonable quality and which are cheaper than national brands, at the lowest cost possible. Indeed, a veritable product of a mature era with low growth on the cards. That said, consumers begun to typically view PB brands in terms of "you get what you pay for," gradually moving away from them. Only MUJI took the trouble to have consumers understand why their brands are low-cost. Rather than attempting to rationalize why they could "offer department store quality goods at 70 percent of the price," MUJI positioned its products as being the "antithesis of a consumer society."

Avoid throwing away foods that are perfectly edible just for the sake of presentation. Use uniform packaging, providing there is no impact on quality. Offer clothing products without starching or ironing, even minus the packaging. "Lower-priced for a reason." Then, sublimate the characteristics of uncompromising simplicity and unpretentiousness into the brand, and roll it out. The intention, however, was never to attract customers merely through cutting costs, simplifying packaging and offering lower prices. Despite being a private brand, costs were not cut for design – in fact, MUJI engaged The late Ikko Tanaka - the leading graphic designer in Japan at the time – to create designs that are still in use to this day. The proposing of a constitutive minimalism rooted in Japanese culture, steeped in the sense of values inherent in Zen and the tea ceremony. This was the essence of MUJI devised by wunderkind marketer Seiji Tsutsumi, also renowned as an author and poet.

In 1983, MUJI - which until then existed within The Seiyu Ltd. – opened its first directly managed street level store in Tokyo's Aoyama District. An employee of The Seiyu Ltd. at that time, Matsui was astonished how sharply the business grew.

"Business was just booming, to the point that we could reach our yearly target in one month."

Feeling an unmistakably firm tug on its line, MUJI became independent from The Seiyu Ltd. in 1989, and wasted no time in venturing overseas.

1991 – MUJI Opens First Overseas Store in London

Seiji Tsutsumi, creator of the MUJI concept, was going to great pains to send personnel abroad and pioneer overseas brands exclusive to Seibu Department Stores in an attempt to boost Seibu's business to the top level; despite being the flagship of the Saison Group, they were late to the game.

The concept of MUJI came to the attention of a person in charge at long-established department store Liberty, Seibu Department Store's business partner in London. This concept would certainly go down very well in Europe. This meant that Seibu – traditionally importers of global brands into Japan – was now being asked if they could export into Europe.

Seiji Tsutsumi knew in his heart that a brand that could not prevail overseas would definitely not survive in Japan.

Just 10 years after MUJI began, and a paltry two years since going independent as RYOHIN KEIKAKU, they were now opening a shop in the middle of London. Such swift footwork was attributable to Seiji Tsutsumi's charisma – as well as the fact that Japan was at the peak of its bubble economy.

"Even from an insider's point of view, the sense of speed was astonishing."

1991 saw Matsui temporarily transferred from The Seiyu Ltd. to RYOHIN KEIKAKU; Matsui, who was working on the front line to create a system for human resources and salary calculation, was in awe at the vigor and energy present within Saison Group at the time.

London's West End. In a corner of Liberty's stately three-story wooden building department store annex, MUJI opened its first overseas store. A group of designers including Ikko Tanaka were dispatched to London, and uncompromisingly set about creating the store. Although they started out offering ingredients including *miso* and soy sauce, it was an uphill battle against the local food culture, and gradually they began to specialize in articles of clothing and general lifestyle goods. In the same year and after London, the first Asian store was opened in Hong Kong; following this, a store in Singapore.

In this manner, MUJI had taken the first steps in its overseas expansion, which amounts to 300 stores today.

The Glory and Failure of Saison

As well as progressive designers from the UK, MUJI also found favor with the refined and forward-looking demographic. These people could sense Japan within MUJI, and eagerly incorporated it into their lifestyles. In Asia too, the reception was wildly enthusiastic. However, seven years into overseas expansion in 1997, MUJI still only had a total of 12 stores, five in Europe and seven in Asia.

"We had trouble permeating among general consumers."

Looking back on the second half of the 1990s, Matsui recalls how the Asian Currency Crisis erupted, further exacerbating the situation and leading to a complete withdrawal from Asia in 1998. In Europe also, the consumption framework had begun to change in tone.

"As with Japan, the department store business model had crumbled."

In developed countries where the market had matured, consumers had begun to select goods based on their individual personalities. Thus, solely in pursuit of their own values, consumers began to favor specialist shops, which could meet more precise needs while managing to respond to severe pricing demands. They preferred these specialist stores over department stores which despite being somewhat expensive, offered everything conveniently in one place, while giving easy access to brand values. In this way, every time a category-killer specialist store appears, department stores face an even tougher battle. Facing mediocre numbers, Liberty underwent a management shake-up and cut its ties with MUJI.

Burdened in the first place by the UK's cumbersome contract conditions, MUJI remained mired in the red. Despite this, in a phase where MUJI deployed steady management in its home base of Japan, it was justifiable to keep the UK store running at a loss for the purpose of shoring up investment into the MUJI brand value. The Saison Group, however, had massive debts following the bubble bursting, beleaguered by a tempest of restructuring and sale of assets.

In 2001, the Saison Group actually dismantled. RYOHIN KEIKAKU was a leading performer among the group's companies, but had run up losses from overseas withdrawals and recorded a 3.8 billion yen deficit in the interim phase of that year.

"It is not at all the case that the journey here has been straightforward."

It was indeed in 2001 that Matsui assumed the position of CEO.

Re-constructing the "Winning Configuration"

Matsui, who was in charge of revamping the business, recalls a very caustic remark from a top analyst at that time.

"Once a specialist shop goes down, it can never recover." When I thought about past cases, I realized that this was true; even if there were stopgap measures, I could not recall one case where there was a completely successful turnaround."

When in the red, restructure first of all. Compress outlay, cut down on personnel expenses, close stores running a deficit. But will it ever be possible to reconstruct the "winning configuration" needed to win back consumers to the merit of MUJI?

Matsui keep asking himself the question.

"I came to wonder whether the "Saison culture" which had spawned MUJI, was actually a shackle."

As well as taking Seibu Department Stores to great heights, Saison again and again came up with visionary business categories such as Parco and Family Mart, as well as MUJI. Despite this, the capability to scientifically pursue operations was definitely weak.

"With department stores, the onus is on individual shops. Each individual store needs to conspicuously display its charm, and so you have to take the initiative in remodeling to ensure that you are constantly elevating their communication. This is the antithesis to operating a chain."

Needless to say, at the forefront of this was genius marketer, Seiji Tsutsumi. You only need one genius. Those around need to wait for his cues, read into what he is saying, keep their opinions to themselves and do their jobs through implicit knowledge. This was a unique approach firmly entrenched in the Saison Group.

In a time of soaring profits, this is all fine as long as the genius is present. However, if excessive individualism or experientialism run rampant, there is the risk that the genius will disappear, after which the nucleus of the brand vanishes without trace. Similarly, if a capable manager leaves a store, it will not be long before that store hits the wall; likewise, people under a bad manager can never expect to grow.

The Saison culture that had built a whole era had drifted away from the prevailing retail commerce theory.

Rather than a Top-notch Strategy, Top-notch Execution Ability is Key

The first step of Matsui's reformation was a hard one.
"The responsibility as president feels 20 times greater than that of executive director."

Nowadays, Matsui can talk about it with a smile on his face. He carried out a restructuring, and disposed of 10 billion yen worth of bad inventory. He closed stores in France. Nevertheless, Matsui felt that what he really had to get to grips with was something akin to a culture that does not manifest in superficial numbers. Matsui set about trying to radically cure the "big company disease" that had proliferated within RYOHIN KEIKAKU. Due to having become a well-recognized brand, MUJI was infested with a fear of rocking the boat, with complete deference to following precedents.

By nature of being a top-down organization led by a charismatic manager, it was impossible for someone further down the ladder to provide any input. The nail that sticks out gets hammered down, so keep quiet. Fellow employees trading blame with each other.

Matsui was convinced that unless he changed this unique Saison culture and cleaned up the company atmosphere, it would not survive for much longer, no matter how well established the brand appeared to be. This was because they would not be able to keep up with the speed of change, and before long, their ability to make things happen and to communicate outward would weaken.

"Imagine there are two companies, one with a top-notch strategy but second-rate execution ability and one with a second-rate strategy but top-notch execution. It is the latter that will survive. What made sense to Saison was against the tide of common sense."

Matsui began to change from the root the corporate culture that had prevailed within MUJI for over 20 years. He would strengthen the backbone the company, instilling responsibility and execution ability into each employee. To do so, he needed to "systematize all operations," establish a manual and render it visible. And so began the formulation of the 2,000-page "MUJIGRAM" manual which would provide the torque for a dramatic recovery for results.

Strategy Alone Cannot Create a Brand

As well as instructing how to create selling spaces and engage with customers, MUJIGRAM provided a wealth of information that anybody would find reasonable, understand and implement. This included how to tap into customer voices, how to use certain flags to determine additional orders, and based on this how to decide whether to increase or decrease production. This made it possible to homogenize education and training and to clarify responsibilities. Each store was homogenized, and important changes were embedded across the board.

Determination of responsibility was also made clear. Rather than pushing through business solely based on MUJI's image, a corporate culture was established that placed a lot of importance on concepts combined with the execution ability to transform these concepts into results.

"A brand, even if you have a superb strategy and concepts, will be nothing without execution ability."

No matter how many times you multiply it by zero, zero will remain zero. While prizing concepts that were a source of charisma, you need to develop the capability to put them into action. It was this approach that became the cornerstone that reinforced the MUJI brand and allowed it to continue.

In 2002, MUJI was back in the black. It has enjoyed increased revenues for 12 consecutive years up until the period ending February 2015, with forecasts that operating profit will exceed the 30 billion yen markbefore long. Within these figures, overseas sales for the period ending February 2015 were approximately 77 billion yen, with astonishing projections that at this rate the period through February

2016 will see sales of 100 billion yen. The number of stores in Asia, of which there were zero at the end of the 1990s, is up to 255 as of the end of October 2015. They continue to significantly contribute to profits.

Matsui ruminates:

"Overseas expansion, however, was wracked with hardships."

He also had a precise approach for reconstructing overseas stores. Concealed within this was the process for MUJI becoming a Japan Brand.

If Forcibly Stretched, a Brand Will Not Grow

Matsui does not deny that establishing the MUJI brand overseas, particularly in the West, is essential for creating the driving force for growth in Japan and in the Asian market. That said, Matsui makes this assertion:

"It takes a long time for a brand to be received by a foreign culture, no matter how good it is. In the interim, it has to remain sustainable as a business."

Put simply, if you wade blindly into Western countries, accruing massive debts just for the sake of giving your brand some added prestige, you may end up actually damaging the value of your brand. This conviction of Matsui's is rooted in a bitter memory.

After withdrawing from Asia and dissolving the tie-up with Liberty, MUJI had to re-launch its overseas expansion completely as it own business. Back in 1998, it was operating 10 stores in Europe. As the Saison Group underwent last-ditch measures to keep it alive, there were people within the group who wanted by all means to maintain the high stock prices of MUJI, one of its leading companies. Making progress in overseas expansion would help raise the value of the brand in Japan, improve the image held by shareholders, while also serving to support a higher stock price. Having established this, the next decision was to significantly increase the number of stores, mainly in France which was progressing relatively well. When Matsui came in as president in 2001, the number of stores in Europe had doubled to 21 – yet for the most part these were in the red.

"We knew at the time it was difficult to target overseas; we went ahead with expansion in spite of this knowledge. Of course, while this may well have improved the MUJI brand value in the short term, the limit would come before long."

Growth Without Quality Only Amounts to Risk

The mere act of growth can never nurture a brand. Despite knowing this, MUJI continued opening stores due to internal factors.

After Matsui became president, it was inevitable that overseas stores would be subject to restructuring. MUJI, however, was starting to make its mark in Europe, albeit slowly. Having become president, Matsui went to work analyzing why so many shops were in the red.

The store in London's bustling shopping district was not doing badly at all in terms of sales. While the price of land in London was high to begin with, the rent there was far too high. Expenses related to personnel and distribution, even if abroad, can be autonomously controlled to an extent. Rent, on the other hand, is fixed under a long-running agreement, which cannot be cancelled further down the track upon the realization that it is too high. Having hurried to open a store, there was no time to scrutinize properties from the perspective of cost-effectiveness, thus rending it impossible to sustainably operate stores that fit a realistic budget.

Despite the existence of core fans and a certain amount of repeat customers, it was not enough to keep the store in the black. Beyond that, in a mature market like Europe, it takes time for a brand to permeate. If a business is to succeed, shops need to be opened in a manner conducive to winning over the long-term.

"Growth without quality is risk, pure and simple," Matsui states flatly.

If possible, all stores should be in the black. While that sounds tough, it is simply not acceptable to expand abroad for the sake of a publicity stunt, while dragging down business results. To remain in the black, rather than unnecessarily expanding in scale, it is preferable to open one store in order to establish a local head office and to cover operating costs, and to then move onto the next store before thinking about expanding into another country. Based on this approach, Matsui closed unprofitable stores that risked staying in the red, while deploying new stores in more economically viable locations.

While withdrawing from unprofitable stores, MUJI also slowly increased the number of stores and countries. Following the UK, France, and Germany, stores were opened in Italy, America, Canada and Australia. This growth spurt led to a total of 73 stores in the U.S. and Europe. These hardships would eventually contribute to huge success in Asia, unmatched by any other brand.

This is How a Peerless Japan Brand was Created

Advances into the West had meant 10 years of hardship. Conversely, in 2001, the year Matsui became president, the company began to reenter Asia, despite having completely withdrawn once. In just 15 years the number of stores grew rapidly to reach 255, growing into a profitable pillar capable of contributing to revenues. What exactly was the reason for MUJI becoming a peerless Japan Brand? Let us return to MUJI's greatest strength as identified by Matsui.

MUJI was, from the outset, firmly rooted in concept and philosophy, and its business category was selling lifestyles. Furthermore, it has remained an SPA throughout. Matsui explained the following conditions required for the MUJI brand to be a global success.

Requirements for Establishing Globalization

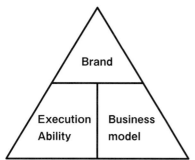

First of all, MUJI places the brand at the top of the pyramid, communicating a philosophy of Japanese origin to consumers and selling them lifestyles. The base supporting the brand consists of execution ability and business model.
Execution ability is underpinned by MUJIGRAM. The business model is SPA.

"We ourselves doing the selling must create products while at the same time understanding the idiosyncrasies of our customers. Doing so will mean a higher success rate and a higher profit ratio."

It is precisely thanks to SPA that the brand's purity goes up. If the brand can permeate, the profit ratio will go up. This was the philosophy that Matsui had identified.

The West and Asia have Very Differing Views of MUJI!

Although MUJI is a brand born in Japan, it is by no means received in a uniform manner. Matsui describes the feeling he got from re-formulating overseas expansion:

"In Europe, MUJI can be likened to 'Kodama.' In Asia, meanwhile, MUJI can be likened to 'Nozomi'." (Kodama is a shuttle-service bullet train, while Nozomi is a super express).

Europe was the first to accept the MUJI concept, yet while some individuals were fervent supporters, they were very much in the minority. In a market where growth has stagnated and where the middle class is increasingly squeezed, management of a high brand is much tougher than Japanese people imagine. While MUJI is well positioned in such a market due to its low unit prices, it was very much a case of a "shuttle-service train" penetrating the market slowly.

Politely enlighten customers, explaining the background to the brand. Thanks to this approach, it was actually possible to elevate the MUJI brand feeling in Europe to a level above Japan, despite unprofitable conditions. What compensated for this was the Asian market, particularly China, experiencing explosive growth in its young middle class.

In contrast to the mature Europe, these markets were full of youngsters with swelling incomes, excited by lifestyles where they could purchase higher quality goods. While it is difficult to construct an original brand, a brand already successful in developed countries is well regarded for its high quality, level of sophistication and sense of reassurance. The speed of penetration was akin to an "super express train."

Matsui continued to boldly open new stores in China, pursuing tie-ups with multiple local companies. These days, MUJI is an indispensable tenant in China's prosperous shopping malls alongside the likes of UNIQLO, ZARA, H&M and Hong Kong drugstore chain Watsons. In Asia, MUJI can be completely accepted into the high-class product category. A brand born in Japan, and refined in Europe. Raising quality of life, and imbued with a philosophy of considering the environment. Such an image of the brand is already established.

How can the Heart of MUJI be Conveyed Overseas?

"In principle, we won't advertise in The U.S. and Europe."

While MUJI is regarded as low-price and functional in Japan, it is considered adesirable brand in The U.S. and Europe. This phenomenon is not only a ttributable to an elevated brand image, but also to the high purchasing power of the customer strata who endorse the MUJI concept - as well as the actual issue facing the supply side of the need to tack on transportation costs. Put simply, one does not casually attempt to enter a market unless there is an understanding and endorsement of the concept at a deep level.

When developing a brand new store, use posters conducive to understanding the MUJI brand, and prepare printed materials. MUJI's cultural background, its history, and its uncompromising approach to making products. Rather than trying to get customers onboard by explaining how it is possible to provide such a lifestyle at such low prices, the aim is to have them appreciate the concept. The company continued to grapple squarely with this aim, albeit unostentatiously, in Pairs, Milan and Dusseldorf.

There are certain things that Matsui warns against. First of all, using pure advertising. In different cultures, the MUJI concept cannot be conveyed through pure advertising. For Matsui, rather than spending on pure advertising, it made more sense to lower prices. Instead of pure advertising, he invited various people from the media and made opportunities to appeal to them in person.

Matsui was equally resolute that while they would leverage the Japan Brand, it was not acceptable to rely on the local Japanese populace or Japanese tourists.

Of course, Japanese are welcome. If the brand does not resound with the local people, however, the business can never last. This is because the more that the world becomes globalized, products and money easily straddle national borders, reducing the motivation to seek out special goods. Maintaining a business in Europe, serving the people who live there who have subtly different cultures and national characteristics. As well as allowing MUJI to take root as a brand, this is linked to the fermenting of an overwhelmingly high-class feel in various Asian countries.

Inner Branding For Local Employees

On another front, it is ultimately the locally hired employees who underpin the execution ability on the front line in overseas MUJI stores. These local hires are key players supporting the MUJI Brand.

In Japan, MUJIGRAM made it possible to robustly systematize everything, allowing standardized manufacturing, sales, management and personnel training. In the U.S. and Europe, however, there was a particular kind of difficulty to grapple with.

To begin with, functions including product planning were stationed in Europe, supplying items in tune with local needs. However, quality control was difficult due to systems not permeating, and at one stage the shelves of these European stores included items far removed from the all-important MUJI concept. "Europe has a proud history, and its people have the mettle to get things done by themselves. If you try and systematize this, however, there is the danger that before long you will end up going the same way that Saison did."

This is Matsui's analysis of the tasks facing the European business in future. In fact, when it comes to embracing systematization things run more smoothly in The U.S. In China, meanwhile, a localized 1,200-page manual equivalent to MUJIGRAM already exists. Given that there are 30 new shops opened every year, bringing in 700-800 new employees, while incorporating local systems it will be important to render work visible and systematize it in order to secure execution ability. The content is also regularly updated. China differs from Japan in that its society revolves around rugged individualism. Naturally, commercial practices differ, and one cannot expect an organization where the store manager and staff members all work together towards a difficult problem. That said, what Chinese consumers ultimately expect from MUJI is quality akin to that of Japan. This led to commending employees who made suggestions to improve MUJIGRAM on an individual basis – rather than on a store basis – and making necessary adjustments in order to retain the Japan Brand, but in a Chinese manner, from management through to personnel training. In this vein, the ascent and expansion of MUJI continues.

How to make a Japan Brand Prevail

Matsui had successfully developed a down-to-earth business that is the flagship of the Japan Brand. I asked for his outlook for Japan Brands and for his advice for others who may seek to follow in his footsteps.
"The appreciation of Japan Brands has become polarized."
UNIQLO and DAISO, TOTO's hygienic porcelain and Daikin's air conditioners. Equally, Ajisen Ramen – are all building up stronger brands overseas. The brand value of Japanese consumer electronics companies, meanwhile, are rapidly deteriorating. Where exactly does the discrepancy lie?
"It comes down to whether the brand can take root in that place, and if it can accept localization. I think this is the key point."
You will not prevail by simply bringing in a Japanese brand as it is. Japan stalwart a certain major udon chain floundered in the Chinese market, apparently due to the texture of its noodles. The extent to which you can localize while retaining the original concept is a major factor for success. Given that MUJI is so massively successful in China and Asia, there are questions as to whether they should dedicate themselves exclusively to this region. Matsui, however, resolutely repudiated this.

"Taking on Asia, with its relatively similar tastes, would surely be the realistic management decision. However, I believe that it is precisely a brand that has prevailed in The U.S. and Europe that has the potential to take the world by storm."

In a Europe dogged by low growth, the business models of Chanel and Gucci are still going strong. This is thanks to leveraging the brand they have cultivated up until now to remain competitive in global markets. This is not something confined to high-end brands - ZARA and IKEA, who managed to grow serving a middle-class facing severe economic conditions, capitalize on their brand image cultivated in Europe to succeed around the world. Matsui explains:

"If you are in two minds about it, it is better to just take the risk and go overseas, preferably one store to begin with, in a developed country. No matter much homework you do from afar, unless you make the actual move you will never know just how demanding it all is. Whether you can remain profitable there, will surely be the first step towards constructing a global brand."

An advance into the Indian market was recently announced. As pioneer of the Japan Brand, all eyes are on MUJI's next move.

Profile of Tadamitsu Matsui
1949: Born in Shizuoka, Japan
1973: Graduated Tokyo University of Education (currently University of Tsukuba), The Faculty of Physical Education. After the graduation, started his career at Seiyu Store Co. Ltd. (currently Seiyu GK).
1992: Transferred to RYOHIN KEIKAKU Co., Ltd. VP of General Affairs/Human Resources, Sr. EVP of MUJI Division
2001: President
2008: Chairman
May 21, 2015: Honorary Advisor

Special Interview | Ryohin Keikaku Former Chairman | Tadamitsu Matsui

ジャパン・ブランドの挑戦01

リラクゼーションを新たなジャパン・ブランドに！

りらく取締役会長
竹之内教博（ゆきひろ）

代表取締役社長兼CEO
出上幸典（いでうえ）

リラクゼーション業界に、
業態と価格の両面から革命を起こした「りらく」。
その次なる一手は、「思い」のブランド化だった。

創設わずか5年で400店舗を達成するという、
怒涛の成長を見せた「りらく」。
驚異的なスピードの原動力、そしてリラクゼーションが映す
新しい可能性と、ジャパン・ブランドを背負った海外展開計画。
そのすべてを、竹之内会長、出上社長が語った。文中、敬称略

The Ascent of The Japan Brand 01

MAKING RELAXATION INTO A NEW JAPAN BRAND!

Chairman, riraku Co.,LTD.
Yukihiro Takenouchi

President and and CEO., riraku Co.,LTD.
Yukinori Ideue

riraku revolutionized the relaxation industry both in terms of business scope and price. The next step will be to turn it into a "feeling" brand.

Opening 400 stores in just five years since establishment, riraku grew in leaps and bounds.
The driving force behind this astonishing speed, new possibilities projected by relaxation, and overseas expansion plans that are carrying the Japan brand – Chairman Takenouchi and CEO Ideue reveal all.

それは美容室から始まった

　りらくという企業について、特筆すべき項目は数多い。が、まず注目しなければならないのは、その驚くべき成長のスピードの速さだろう。

　開業は2009年。大阪・和泉市で、現会長の竹之内教博ともうひとりの創業者で始めた事業は、6年で日本全国に400店舗以上を展開する業界トップ級の企業に成長した。

　創業当時の思い出を、竹之内に聞いた。

「私はもともと大手ヘアカラーメーカーに所属して、美容室やサロンのコンサルティングをしていました。美容室の経営改善に取り組むうち、私が個人的に好きだったリラクゼーションサロンの業態を試しに導入してみたところ手応えを感じて、手作りでお店を始めたのがきっかけでした」

　もともと経営的に苦しい状況を打開するために生まれたアイデア。当然、初期投資はそれほどできない。喫茶店、エステ、ホワイトニングなど、さまざまな業態に転換して苦戦していた美容室を、リラクゼーションサロンに改装していった。勝負できる材料は、とりあえず価格競争力しかない。そこで、当時の相場のほぼ半値に当たる60分2980円というコンセプトを打ち出したところ、思った以上に好感触を得ることができた。やがて業容が拡大してくると、できるだけ居抜きに近い、初期投資のかからない物件を求めて全国を奔走する。その積み重ねが、450店舗（2015年11月末時点）。しかも、すべて直営なのだという。マッチングという新しい考え方をリラクゼーション業界に取り入れ、顧客の支持を集め続けているりらく。今後は上場だけでなく、海外進出を視野に入れている。

　その成長力と可能性を探ってみたい。

It All Started from a Beauty Salon

There are many things worthy of mention regarding riraku. First of all, however, it is surely the sheer speed at which it grew that merits particular attention.

The business was established in 2009. Launched in Izumiotsu-City in Osaka by current Chairman Takenouchi and one other founder, the business opened over 400 stores throughout Japan in six years, making it a top company in the industry.

Takenouchi shares his memories of the early days.

"I was originally part of a major hair color manufacturer, doing consulting for hairdressers and beauty salons. Working on improving management of such salons, I experimentally introduced the business category of relaxation salon - which I personally liked - and felt a good response; that was the catalyst to start putting together my own home-made stores."

An idea that sprang from a need to overcome tough management conditions. Naturally, early-stage investment was limited. He began remodeling floundering beauty salons that had switched to various business categories - including coffee shops, esthetic clinics, and teeth whitening salons - into relaxation salons. Price competitiveness was the only means available for winning out amongst the competition. When he pioneered the concept of charging 2,980 yen for an hour – nearly half the going rate at the time – the response was greater than he expected. Before long, as operations began to expand, he scrambled around Japan looking for potential properties that were already furnished and which would require no initial investment. These stacked up to 450 stores(as of the end of November 2015). What is more, these were all directly managed. Incorporating the new concept of "matching" into the relaxation industry, riraku continues to enjoy support from customers. As well as listing on the stock exchange, riraku may well expand overseas.

I would like to explore this vitality and potential.

急成長の原動力

　しかし、どうすればこのようなスピード感のある経営が可能になるのだろうか。私の知る限り、日本一といっていいほど経営判断が迅速で、しかも未だとどまるところを知らない。2010年に現在の会社を設立。翌年夏に70店舗、2012年初めには100店舗を超え、同年末には200店舗、2013年末300店舗、そして2015年4月に400店舗を達成した。怒涛、といっても過言ではない成長ぶりである。しかも、本社機能は極めてコンパクトだ。

　社長兼CEOの出上幸典は言う。
「本部の社員は全部で100人程度です。そのうち40人程度は経理ですから、店舗開発はより少数精鋭ですよ」

　それだけの速さで成長しながら、経営的な齟齬は今のところほとんどないという事実にも驚かされる。

　竹之内は静かに語る。
「りらくは、初期投資の減価償却を除けば、単月単位で赤字の店舗はほとんどありません」

　つまり、それだけりらくというブランドが顧客に支持されているという証左だ。その秘密を聞いてみると、竹之内からはこんな答えが返ってきた。
「仕事をしてくれるセラピスト様が、環境的にも金銭的も働きやすいこと。そして利益が出ればできるだけお客様に還元していくこと。加えて、セラピスト様もお客様も喜べる場所を選んで出店するようにしています。家賃が高すぎれば価格設定を見直さなければならないし、営業時間に制約があればそれだけ機会が減ってしまいます。ただ価格設定を安くすればいいというのではなく、利用する人が何を望んでいるかを考えながらすべての決定を下しています」

The Driving Force behind Rapid Growth

First of all, what exactly makes such speedy management possible? As far as I am aware, their management decisions are as swift as any other in Japan, and are certainly not running out of steam.

The company as it exists today was established in 2010. In the following year they had 70 stores, and by early 2012 this rose to 100 and then to 200 by the end of the year, rising up further to 300 at the end of 2013 and reaching 400 stores by April 2015.

It is no exaggeration to say that these were surging waves of growth. What is more, the headquarters' function is extremely compact.

Representative Director and CEO Yukinori Ideue explains:
"There are approximately 100 employees in the head office. About 40 of these are in accounting, meaning that it is just a select few who handle store development."

Another astonishing fact is that they were able to peg such rapid growth with hardly any major management disagreements.

Takenouchi quietly explains:
"riraku, excluding initial investment depreciation, hardly has any stores in the red on a single month basis."

Put simply, this is evidence of just how much customers endorse the riraku brand. When asked about the secret to this, Takenouchi gave the following reply:
"Making sure that the therapists who work for us feel comfortable both in terms of environment and financial compensation. When we make a profit, we return it to our customers wherever possible. In addition, we try to open new shops in locations that will please both customers and therapists. If the rent is too high, we have to revise our pricing structure, and if there are limits on opening hours then we lose opportunities as a result. Beyond just setting the price as low as we can, all decisions are made by carefully thinking about what

常識を壊したロードサイド戦略

　読者の中には、りらくのことを知らない人がいるかもしれない。恐らくその人は、都心部からあまり出ることがなく、クルマに乗らない生活をしているのではないだろうか。一方で、関東でもクルマの利用が便利な郊外や、各地方都市では、りらくの知名度は圧倒的に高い。黄色い看板の、2980円のりらくと聞けば、すぐに数ヵ所の店舗の場所が思い浮かぶ。そのくらい、日々の生活に浸透し始めているのだ。

　もともと、りらくが急成長する以前のリラクゼーション業界は、駅前のビルに店舗を構える業態が一般的だった。りらくも、当初は同様だったという。しかし、早々に方針を転換した。というより、せざるを得なかった。低価格でも利益を出すには、極力手間とコストをかけないことが肝要だ。ならば、家賃の比較的高い駅前はひとまず敬遠し、駐車場の広く取れるロードサイド型の店舗を展開したほうがいい。そうした業態のリラクゼーションは、当時ほぼ皆無だったという。竹之内はその内幕を教えてくれた。

「実を言うと、ビルインの店舗のほうが人材は集めやすく、ロードサイドのほうが苦労します。これは裏を返すと、ビルインのほうが参入障壁が低く、いわばありふれた業態なのに対して、ロードサイドは面倒な分手付かずで、私の眼には早い者勝ちのように映ったのです」

　400店舗にまで拡大した現在でも、ロードサイド型の比率は8割以上を占めている。ということは、日々クルマを使って生活している人にとっては、りらくが間違いなくナンバーワンの知名度、信頼度を誇るブランドになり得ているということになる。セラピストとして働くことを考える際も、まずりらくを思い起こしてもらえる。それが、間断なき急成長を支えている「非常識」な経営なのだ。

our customers are looking for in terms of service."

"Roadside" Strategy Contrary to Common Sense

There may be some readers among you who have never heard of riraku. These people, presumably, rarely leave the center of town and do not use a car in their daily lives. Meanwhile, in suburbs suited for car usage in the Kanto region and in various regional cities, riraku is overwhelmingly well known. On hearing about the yellow sign and the 2,980 yen per hour riraku, the location of several stores will come to mind. Such is the degree to which it is permeating daily lifestyles.

In the days before riraku grew to great heights, the relaxation industry was typified by a business style of having stores in buildings that adjoin major stations. Indeed, riraku started out in this fashion. However, they quickly transformed their plan. To be precise, they had no choice but to. Making a profit at low prices is all about avoiding expending time and money wherever possible. In which case, it makes sense to pass up buildings by stations that are relatively high in rent, and to select roadside stores with plenty of parking space. Such a type of relaxation business was almost non-existent at that time. Takenouchi provides the lowdown:

"To be honest, stores inside a large building are easy from the point of view of recruiting staff, while the opposite is true of roadside stores. Put another way, compared to large buildings, which have low obstacles to entry and are somewhat commonplace, stores by the roadside, while being a hassle to organize, represent an untapped opportunity so it seemed to me like a case of whoever gets there first."

Today when they have expanded to 400 stores, the ratio of roadside type stores is over 80percent. What this signifies is that for people who use cars on a daily basis, riraku has become number one brand both in terms of level of recognition and reliability. Therapists too, associate riraku with being the

毎週2店舗出店の舞台裏

　りらくの出店ペースは、年間約100店舗。つまり、おおむね週2店舗のペースである。2015年7月、最後まで出店していなかった山形県に1号店を開業、全47都道府県への出店を達成した。そこに至る道筋は、いわゆるドミナント戦略である。

「今日は東京、明日は名古屋とやっていたのでは、業態がシンプルだけに隙間に入り込まれてしまう。当社の評判が良ければ良いほど、近くにライバル企業の店舗出現を招いてしまいます。そこで、県ごと、それも地域や沿線単位で集中的に物件をリサーチし、間を開けずに出店する戦略を取ったのです」

　竹之内の戦略は、シンプルでありながら理にかなっていて、しかも実行力に優れていた。ロードサイドを徹底調査し、コストの安い居抜き物件を中心に精力的に調査した。特に、広い駐車場が取れるコンビニの居抜き物件に注目した。もともと広く一般の消費者の集客を考えて出店したところだから、より専門的な業態であるリラクゼーションとしては必要十分な条件が揃っているケースが多かったのだ。そして、ドミナントで展開を行うことで、開店準備を整える際にも、本社から送り込むスタッフは効率良く準備をすることができる。こうして、アイデアが真似されないうちに、面で商圏を押さえることができる。ある時から急に、たびたびりらくの看板を眼にするようになって、価格設定のインパクトとブランドが強く結びつく——。それが狙いだったのだ。

　一方で、外装や看板、広告宣伝といった経費は極力絞り込み、オープン当初のチラシと口コミ、そしてインターネットに限った。成長の過程で、直接価値を生み出さないものに投資しても、結局負担するのは顧客であり、セラピストである。成功しても実利的な投資しかしないりらくの企業文化は、純粋で、徹

number one place to work. This is the "unconventional common sense" management underpinning uninterrupted rapid growth.

Behind the Scenes of Opening Two New Stores Per Week

riraku opens new stores at a rate of approximately 100 per year. In other words, this works out to roughly two new stores every week. In July 2015, riraku opened their first store in the hitherto untapped Yamagata Prefecture, and in doing so achieved the feat of opening a store in each of the 47 prefectures. The path leading up to this point was the so-called dominant strategy.

"If we expanded step by step opening one store in Tokyo today and then Nagoya tomorrow, because the business is simple, competitors might wedge themselves into our spots. The better our company's reputation became, the more that rival company stores started to appear nearby. At that point, we adopted a strategy of intensively researching properties by prefecture, train line, and region, promptly opening stores one after another."

While simple, Takenouchi's strategy stood to reason and was excellent in terms of execution capability. He thoroughly investigated "roadside" areas and dynamically searched for cheap properties, principally those that came with all the furnishings. In particular, he focused on convenience stores with large parking areas that were being sold with furniture and fixtures included. Given that these stores themselves were originally set up with the intention of drawing in swathes of general consumers, many had in place the necessary conditions for the relaxation business, which is though more specialist than convenience stores. This dominant manner of expanding means that when it comes to preparations for opening a store, staff can be dispatched from head office to ensure efficient preparations. In this way, a company can dominate a local market by opening stores there and catering to customer needs before the idea is imitated by someone else. Then one day, all of sudden people

底されていた。

顧客とセラピストが出会う場所

りらくでセラピストとして働いているスタッフは、すべて業務委託契約だ。りらくの雇用する従業員ではない。つまり、りらくの従業員ではないスタッフが、りらくの従業員ではない顧客に施術を行うスタイルだ。各スタッフは、りらくと業務委託契約を交わした「取引先」であり、個人事業主である。そして、セラピスト個々人が、りらくの店舗にあるスペースや設備を借りて営業を行うという形式を取っている。もちろん、そこに指揮系統、命令系統は存在しないし、各店に店長もいない。店長はいなくとも、りらくのセラピストはプロフェッショナルの集まりだ。事実、同業他社からりらくへ転職したセラピストからは「りらくのセラピストは顧客志向を持った人が多い」という声がよくあがっている。「お客様の身体を楽にしてあげたい」、その一心で、独学やセラピスト間のコミュニケーションにて知識量を増やし、技術力にも磨きをかけている。さらには、お客様の身体の状態や施術内容をノートにまとめて自己管理するなど、お客様にずっと寄り添っ

大阪府泉大津市にある本社。100人近くの社員が驚異的な成長を支えている

Headquartered in Izumiotsu-City, Osaka. Just under 100 employees support astounding growth.

start to notice riraku signs, and the impact of the pricing structure and brand became strongly linked in people's minds. This was what riraku was aiming for.

Meanwhile, expenses such as exterior/signs and advertising were kept to an absolute minimum, limited to flyers and word of mouth when opening a store, as well as using the Internet. In the growing process, investing in things that do not directly produce value means that ultimately it is the customer and therapists who shoulder the cost. Sticking to pragmatic investing even when successful, the corporate culture of riraku was simple and thorough.

A Place Where Customers and Therapists Come Together

Therapists working at riraku are all employed through outsourcing agreements. In other words, under this arrangement, staff who are not riraku employees practice on customers who are not riraku employees. Each member of staff is a "business partner" who has exchanged an outsourcing agreement with riraku, doing business as a sole proprietor. Each individual therapist borrows space and amenities within a riraku salon to carry out their operations. Needless to say, there is no chain of command system, and there is no manager in each store. Even in the absence of a manager, riraku therapists are a highly professional group. In actual fact, therapists joining riraku from competitor companies often comment that: "riraku therapists tend to be very customer-focused." With the united desire to provide relief to the bodies of their customers, therapists increase their level of knowledge through self-study and also by communicating with other therapists, enabling them to polish their techniques. They also keep detailed notes regarding their regular customers' conditions and the type of treatment they administered, in order to always be there for their customers when needed. Rather than being coerced by somebody, each individual riraku therapist remains independent and able

ていくために、誰かに強要されることなく、個々人が自立し、自分らしさを活かしながら、高い意欲と強い意志でお客様満足を追求しているのがりらくのセラピストだ。セラピストと契約を締結する段階で、ブランドイメージを汚さない接客マナーや、一般的な社会人としての人柄を見るが、施術面、サービス面でどのような営業を行うかは、あくまでセラピスト本人次第ということになる。

売上の中から、施設の使用料として一定の額をりらくに納めてもらい、残りはセラピスト本人が手にする。給与ではなく報酬であり、税務申告もあくまでセラピストの手によることになる。企業としてのりらくが提供している本質的価値は、いわば「顧客とセラピストの出会いの場」、つまりマッチングなのだ。

竹之内は、この仕組みを起業当初から想定していた。

「たくさんの美容室と接した経験から、店長さんが美容師の扱いに苦労する姿を頻繁に見てきました。本来美容師は一人ひとりできることも得意分野も違いますし、顧客は美容師を指名することができますから、形態としてはかなり個人事業主に近い。りらくも店長を置かず、セラピスト様それぞれが対等の立場で良い場所を互いに保ちながら、自分の努力によって顧客を獲得していく姿が自然ではないかと考えたのです」

顧客はセラピストを指名できるし、顧客に支持されているセラピストはりらくのHPに掲載される。こうして、店舗の出会いの場としての価値が、ますます高まっていく。

三者Win-Win

こうしたりらくの業態は、三者のWin-Winの価値を生み出すことになった。まず、顧客はこれまででは考えられないような低価格でプロ意識の高いセラピス

to inject their own self into their work, aiming for customer satisfaction through high ambition and strong determination. At the stage of concluding a contract with a therapist, riraku makes sure that they possess customer service skills and will not tarnish the brand image, ensuring that they have a satisfactory manner of dealing with people. However, it is ultimately up to the therapist to decide what they practice or what sort of service they will provide to customers.

Therapists pay a certain amount of money from sales proceeds to riraku as a facilities usage fee, but keep the rest. This is not salary, but financial compensation; therapists are responsible for declaring their own taxes.

The essential value that riraku is providing as a corporation is "a place where customers and therapists come together," in other words, matching.

This framework is what Takenouchi had in mind when he started the company:
"From my experience working with lots of hair salons, I often saw store managers struggling to deal with their practitioners. In the first place, practitioners (stylists) all have different strengths and specialties, and customers can specify which practitioner they want – as such, the arrangement is already close to that of a self-employed person. There are no managers in riraku stores, as I felt it was more natural for therapists to be on an equal footing with each other and to mutually create a good space to work in, gaining customers through their own hard work."

Customers may specify which therapist they want, and therapists popular with customers are featured on the riraku website. And in this way, the value of the store as a place of encounters keeps going up and up.

A Win-Win-Win Arrangement

In this way, riraku's business model created value that was a win for all three parties. First of all, customers are able to receive treatment from highly

トの施術を受けることができる。駅前に店舗はないかもしれないが、クルマさえ運転できればアクセスには困らないし、足を伸ばすだけの価格訴求力がある。

りらくの集客力は非常に高く、途切れることなく顧客が来店することで、「同業他社と比べ、技術を磨く機会が豊富であり、技術力の向上が早い」と感じるセラピストが多いのだろう。セラピストは、りらくのブランドによってたくさんの顧客との出会いが期待できるだけでなく、努力によって「自分の顧客」にしようというモチベーションが働く。これが、顧客の満足度をさらに上げることは言うまでもない。そしてりらくは、この仕組みを提供し、ブランドイメージを保つ仕事に特化して、できるだけローコストで運営できるよう必要十分かつ最低限の運営だけを行うことができる。

「全国400店舗に、コンビニエンスストアのようなスーパーバイザーがついていて、店内の清潔さや、外装、幟(のぼり)などのチェックを定期的に行っています。これは9人で分担しています」

9人！ 社長の出上は、事も無げに語る。そこまでコストを削減しても、とどまらない店舗展開を実現できているというのだから、驚かされる。その分、価格は下げられる。価格が下がれば、来店数も増える。こうして、三者三様のメリットが生み出されていくのだ。一方で、価値を生み出す瞬間である施術の技術向上には人材を惜しまない。りらくは全国に50人以上の「先生役」を確保していて、セラピストはオープン前を中心に細かい指導を受けられる体制が整えられている。これは、短期的にはりらく店内において行われる施術の価値向上のためだが、セラピストの立場からは、自身のキャリア開発のための機会を与えられることに他ならない。人材確保がますます難しくなってくる中で、こうした施策にはコストを惜しまないことが大切なのだ。

professional therapists at a low price that was previously unthinkable. There may not be any stores right in front of a station, but as long as you have a car then access is no problem, and the services represents such good value that people are happy to go the extra mile to get there.

   riraku has an extremely high ability to attract customers. Presumably, therapists feel that an uninterrupted inflow of customers afford them many opportunities to polish their techniques as therapists - compared to other competitor companies - enabling them to swiftly raise their level of competence. For therapists, rather than expecting to meet lots of customers through the strength of the riraku brand, there is the motivation to endeavor to cultivate "their own customers." Naturally, this further increases the level of satisfaction among customers. In providing this system, riraku can focus exclusively on maintaining the brand image, only implementing the bare minimum of administration necessary to keep operating costs as low as possible.

"Each of our 400 stores countrywide is assigned a supervisor, akin to the kind you have in a convenience store, who regularly checks the store for cleanliness, exterior, banners and so on. This work is handled by nine employees.

   Nine employees! CEO Ideue speaks as though this is no big deal. Equally surprising is that despite such unrestrained cost-cutting, it was possible to continue to open new stores. To that extent, prices can be kept low. If prices can be kept low, more customers will come. This ensures that merit is created for each of the three respective parties. Meanwhile, no effort is spared in deploying human resources to enhance the techniques of practitioners who create value at each moment. riraku retains over 50 "mentor teachers" around the nation, as part of its framework for providing detail-oriented instruction - mainly for therapists - before a store is opened. While in the short term this raises the value of practice carried out in riraku stores, from the point of view of therapists, it is unmistakably an opportunity to develop their careers. As it becomes increasingly hard to secure human resources, it is important to spare

リラクゼーションは社会に貢献する

　リラクゼーションとは、もちろん医療ではないし、治療行為でもない。だが、そのことは十分承知の上で、日本の長寿社会に貢献できる大切な機能を担えるのではないかと思う。顧客は、意識的にせよ無意識的にせよ、自分のこれからの暮らしをより豊かにするためには「自分自身で進んで気をつけることが必要だ」と感じ取り始めている。ここに、身体だけでなく、心も健やかになれるノウハウの要素も、加えて良いかもしれない。

　身体と心のヘルスケア。その両面が揃うことの重要性。そして「気づき」の促しと、健康になるための「学び」。これらがセットになった状態を、りらくでは一生を通じての「ライフケア」と呼んでいる。私には、その状態こそが、本当の「健康」だと思えるのだ。「りらく」はサービスであると同時に、気づきの「場」でもある。

　IT技術の進歩で人々の生活も変わり、PCやスマホによる眼の疲れや肩こりだけでなく、さらには人との関わり合いで生まれる「ストレス」が身体の不調を招いている。身体の健康と心の健康は密接につながっているのだ。そして、直接顧客の肌に触れる関係性が成立しているからこそできる、リラクゼーションのまだ見ぬ価値と社会貢献への可能性が、りらくには隠されている。私はそう信じている。

働きやすさを追求すれば、顧客も満足する

　りらくの経営が軌道に乗ってくるにつれて、行き着いたひとつの答えがある。当初は、なるべく手間のかからず、リスクの少ない業態を探してたどり着いたス

no expense in measures such as these.

Relaxation Contributes to Society

Relaxation is, needless to say, not medical care, and neither is it therapeutic practice. However, I do believe that with that knowledge in mind, it does play an important function that can contribute to Japan's longevity society. Whether consciously or subconsciously, customers are beginning to sense that "taking the initiative in being responsible for your own well-being" is important in order to enrich their future lifestyles. This could also be said to include elements of know-how for having a healthy and enriched mind.

Healthcare for body and mind: the importance that both of these are present. Furthermore, the encouragement of "recognizing" and "learning" in order to become healthy. riraku refers to the melding of these elements as "life care" throughout the course of one's life. To me, it is precisely this state that can be deemed to be genuinely healthy. As well as providing a service, riraku is a place where people can "recognize."

Progress in IT technology has changed people's lives, and as well as the tired eyes and shoulders resulting from PC and smartphone use, people also experience physical stress caused by mental strain from interactions with other people. Physical health and mental health are closely interlinked. Hidden in riraku are the possibilities for social contribution and the value of relaxation that is yet undiscovered and made possible by being able to come into direct contact with customers.

Ensuring a Pleasant Working Environment Will also Satisfy Customers

Once the management of riraku was well under way, a certain realization transpired. At the outset, a search for a business model with little hassle and low risk led them to a certain style of operating. However, in the process

タイル。しかし、工夫を重ねるうちに、自らの事業が大きな社会性を担っていることに気づいたという。

竹之内は、こう語ってくれた。

「セラピスト様には、それこそ東大や京大を卒業した人もいれば、個人で開業している人、かつて開業していた人、これから開業を目指す人もいます。通常のパートでは働きにくい主婦の方もいらっしゃいます。りらくの、長時間営業、セラピスト様の出勤自由という業態が、実は頑張りたいけれどさまざまな事情を抱えている人の、大切な受け皿になっていると思うのです」

セラピストは業務委託契約であり、あらかじめ断れば何時から何時まで働いても自由である。しかもりらくの営業時間は、基本的に朝10時から深夜2時30分となっているため、選択の余地は幅広い。本業としても副業としても、空き時間活用としても適しているし、自分の都合によってシフトを調整できる。全国で契約しているセラピストは、およそ8000人。そのすべてが頻繁に施術をしているわけではないが、複数の店を掛け持ちする人もいる。家庭の事情で引っ越さなければならなくなっても、引っ越し先のりらくでスムーズに働けるケースも少なくない。本部からの、シフトの空き具合を知らせるメールに応じて、スト

りらくのセラピストは個人事業主のため、比較的自由に働くことが可能
As independent contractors, riraku therapists can work relatively freely.

of refining this business style, they came to realize that their business was shouldering an important social element.

Takenouchi provided an explanation:

"Among therapists, there are those who graduated from universities like Tokyo and Kyoto, those who are opening a business as an individual, those who once opened a business, and those who are aiming to open a business in future. There are also housewives who find it hard to work at conventional part-time jobs. I believe that riraku's business configuration, with its extended opening hours and freedom of attendance at work for therapists, is actually a valuable safety net for people who want to work hard but cannot for various reasons."

Therapists are employed on outsourcing service agreements, giving them the freedom to work whatever hours they like, if they specify in advance. On top of this, riraku salons are basically open from 10a.m. till 2:30a.m., providing a large window to choose from. It could be a main job or a side job, and is also suited to using up spare time; therapists can adjust their shifts to fit their needs. There are approximately 8,000 contracted therapists throughout Japan. It is not the case they are all frequently practicing, and some therapists work at several different salons. It is not at all rare to hear about therapists who had to move house for various reasons and could easily find work at a riraku near their new place of residence. Apparently, therapists also appreciate being able to decide working hours in a stress-free manner thanks to emails from head office regarding available shifts.

"In every sense, we are aiming to provide the top level of satisfaction for therapists. The busiest and most ambitious therapists really appreciate the level of freedom we offer."

What Takenouchi says might sound a little odd to begin with, given that he is not talking about customer levels of satisfaction. However, if the therapists are happy in their working environment, this will most certainly project onto the customers.

レスフリーで出勤時間を決められるのも好評だという。

「すべては、セラピスト様満足度ナンバーワンを目指してしていることなのです。頑張っているセラピスト様ほど、当社の自由さを気に入ってくれています」

竹之内の言葉は、いきなり字面だけ見ると少し違和感を抱くかもしれない。顧客満足度ではないのだから。しかし、施術を行うセラピストが働きやすければ、確実にそれは顧客に投影されるのだ。

セラピストの満足度を大切にしつつ1000店舗達成へ

出上に、今後の事業展望を聞いた。

「ひとまず、500店舗は目前に見えています。このまま順調に拡大を続ければ、国内だけでも1000店舗は実現できると分析しています。売上も現在200億円規模ですが、1000店舗を実現した際は、シンプルに倍増できると考えています」

竹之内や出上がたびたび触れていたように、この業態は参入障壁が高くない。ライバル企業も店舗数を増やしている。その点に心配はないのだろうか。

出上の観点は少し違う。

「競合が多いという以上に、これからは人材の確保が一段と難しくなってくるでしょう。いざ店舗を増やしたくても、セラピスト様が確保できないのです。当社の強みは、当初からとにかくドミナント戦略を突き通したことで、ブランド名が知れたこと。そしてセラピスト様の満足度を大切にしていることです。ここさえ間違わなければ、ライバルへの対処や、今後の成長もあまり心配することはないと考えています」

もっとも、単に店舗数を競うのであれば、各店の利益を度外視することでさらなる出店は可能なのだという。ただそれでは、セラピストを大切にしてきたこ

Achieving 1,000 Stores While Prioritizing Therapist Satisfaction

I asked Ideue about the future outlook for the business.
"First of all, 500 stores are within our grasp. Our analysis suggests that if we continue our steady expansion on the current track, we can achieve 1,000 stores just in Japan. Current sales are in the region of 20 billion yen; if we make 1,000 stores a reality, I think we can easily double that amount."

As Takenouchi and Ideue touched upon several times, the hurdles to entering this market are not high. Rival companies are also increasing their number of stores. Is he not worried about that?

Ideue has a slightly different perspective.
"Beyond the fact that there is more competition, presumably it will become increasingly difficult to secure employees. Even if you want to increase your number of stores, you can't secure therapists. Our strength comes from having penetrated early on with a dominant strategy, which made our brand well known. Another strength is that we take our therapists level of satisfaction very seriously. If we can just do these things right, I don't think there is any need to worry about fending off rivals and ensuring future growth."

If it comes down to competing over number of stores, it would easily be possible to scale up the number, disregarding the profit of each store. Yet to do so would be at odds with the existing policy of putting therapists first.

With regard to floating the company on the stock exchange, Takenouchi does not feel any pressing need.

"At any rate, we will end up listing at some point. In terms of scale I think we would easily clear the requirements. That said, there are no concrete plans afoot at the moment. Rather than preparing to list, we would rather divert resources towards opening new stores."

I think Takenouchi has shown incredibly good judgment. A stock market debut would certainly have the effect of raising recognition and brand image. However, for a B to C company such as riraku, it is intrinsically more important

れまでの方針と矛盾してしまう。株式の上場についても、竹之内は、差し迫った必要性はないと考えている。

「いずれ間違いなく、上場の方向には行くでしょう。規模の面でも十分クリアできると考えています。ただ、現段階では具体的な準備はしていません。上場のための準備よりも、今は出店にリソースを割いていきたいのです」

竹之内のこの判断はすばらしいと思う。株式上場には、知名度やブランドイメージを向上させる効果が確かに存在する。しかしBtoCのりらくであれば、顧客に対するサービスで正面から名前を知ってもらうほうが、本質的に大切なことなのだ。

ジャパン・ブランドの新たな旗手として

これまで年間100店舗のペースで出店してきたりらくであれば、あと5年あまりで彼らの想定する国内のピーク、1000店舗体制に達してしまう計算になる。そこで、中長期的な目標になってきたのが、海外進出だ。

竹之内の考えはこうだ。

「現在は、まだリサーチをかけている段階です。すでに韓国や台湾、アメリカに出かけ、現地事情の視察を始めています。どんな業態、どんな形というイメージはこれからの課題ですが、まずは遠くない将来に、海外1号店を出したいと考えています」

私は、このスタンス、この志に、全面的に賛成したい。クルマでもテレビでもない、ヘルスケアというサービス、そして「健康」であることの大切さという「想い」を輸出する仕事こそ、これからの日本のキラーコンテンツになると考えているからだ。そして、日本が、日本人が作ってきた「想い」が世界の人々の気

to serve customers in order that they recognize the name head on.

As a New Flag-bearer for the Japan Brand

Having opened new stores to the tune of 100 per year, riraku are on course to achieve their envisioned domestic peak of 1000 stores in Japan in a little over five years. With that, their objective for the medium-term is to expand overseas.

Takenouchi sees it like this:

"At present, we are still in the research phase. We have already been over to Korea, Taiwan and America to get a picture of the current state of affairs. While we still have to decide exactly what form the business would take, in the not-too-distant future we would like to open our first overseas store."

I thoroughly endorse this stance and intention in every respect. I do so because, instead of televisions and cars, the job of exporting a healthcare service and the notion that being healthy is very important, could become extremely valuable export commodities for Japan. Indeed, the idea that a concept devised in Japan and by Japanese people is already starting to captivate the feelings of people around the world, is already evident in the level of satisfaction of travelers.

What is more, in a Japan that is the "country of hospitality," riraku has a track record of sudden growth that is rarely witnessed. In the market that is most insistent on "thoughtfulness" in the world, it is a success story made possible by the overwhelming support of both customers and therapists. Companies with a rock-steady business model such as riraku will surely find fertile markets overseas. While Asia is expected to continue developing economically with increasing demands for high-quality service industries, there are also expectations for a rapidly increasingly aging population, suggesting that Japan-brand healthcare will surely be ushered in eagerly.

Furthermore, based on my experiences, I would love to see riraku seek

持ちをとらえ始めていることは、旅行客の満足度を見ればすでに周知の事実になりつつある。

しかも、「おもてなしの国」日本で、りらくはまれに見る急成長を成し遂げてきた実績がある。世界一「想い」にうるさいマーケットで、顧客にも、セラピストにも圧倒的に支持されたからこそ可能になったストーリーだ。りらくのような、確固としたビジネスモデルを築いている企業であれば、当然海外でもニーズは高いと思われる。今後も経済発展が続き、質の高いサービス業への需要が高まるであろうアジアでは、同時に急速な高齢化も見込まれている。ジャパン・ブランドのヘルスケアは、まさに持ってこいのビジネスになるだろう。

そして、私は自らの経験をもとに、北米での成功の可能性に触れておきたい。特に、国民皆保険とはほど遠いアメリカにおいては、所得の高い層を中心に、健康の自己管理へのニーズは大きい。そしてなんといっても、アメリカは今後も長い間、成長、拡大を続けていくであろう、有望かつ巨大なマーケットだ。

「想い」を次の成長につなげる

日本のリラクゼーションのトップブランドであるりらくは、まずトップブランドであること自体が、海外進出時に強い訴求力を持つはずだ。ただ、すでに同様の業態は海外にも存在している。そこに、「日本のりらく」が出ていき、ジャパン・ブランドとして勝負するには、どのような強みを発揮し、どこをアジャストしていくべきなのだろうか。これは、今後海外進出を考えている日本企業にも共通するテーマであり、課題である。

日本の自動車がすばらしいコストパフォーマンスを発揮していること、あるいは日本のデジタルカメラが世界で最高のクオリティであること、今までは毛嫌いし

out the potential for success in the North American market. In particular, in an America where universal healthcare is still far away, the need for self-administered healthcare, particularly for the higher-income bracket, will be significant. Apart from anything else, America will continue growing and expanding for a long while yet, making it a very attractive and sizeable market.

Connecting "Feeling" into the Next Growth Phase

riraku is the top brand for relaxation in Japan; this fact in itself should be a strong source of appeal power when it comes to advancing overseas. However, the same kind of business category already exists overseas. What sort of strengths should be manifested, and what needs to be adjusted in order for "Japan's riraku" to venture abroad and to succeed as a Japan Brand? This is a theme shared by other Japanese corporations looking to expand abroad, and raises certain issues.

In wealthy countries, it is fair to say that nearly anybody knows about the amazing cost performance of Japanese cars, that Japanese digital cameras are the highest quality in the world, or about the nutritious and delicious taste of raw fish eaten as sushi - which people once shunned. Over time, consumers around the world have come to recognize the quality of Japanese things,

セラピストのスキル向上を図るため、50人以上の講師が細かく指導を行う
To improve the skill of therapists, over 50 instructors provide detailed guidance.

ていた生魚も寿司として食べればおいしくヘルシーであることを、ある程度豊かな国で今や知らない人などいない。世界中のユーザーが、長い時間をかけてモノとしての良さを実感できたからこそ、日本そのものがブランドとなった。一方で、サービス業は、コンセプト、「想い」そのものを、現地の文化や発想にアジャストしながら「輸出」していく必要がある。この作業は、言語や文化の違いが障壁となって、これまではあまり進んでこなかった。

　ここに来てようやく、グローバル化や情報通信技術の発展が、高い障壁を崩し始めている。日本の質の高い「想い」が、本当に伝えられる時代、伝えようと努めれば伝わる可能性の高い時代が始まりつつあるのだ。私たちは、決して国内市場におけるりらくの成長ぶりだけを見て驚いていてはいけない。りらくの真剣な「想い」が伝わり、ブランドの構築に成功すれば、恐らく今までの何倍もの成長が、今後現実のものとなってくるだろう。

国内で伸びる企業は世界でも伸びる

　多くの日本企業、中でも内需型の企業は、今後の国内市場の先行きが明るくないことを悲観している。日本のモノやサービスはクオリティが高いから、とにかく海外に打って出よう、というアドバイスも聞かれる。それ自体は正しい。しかし私は、単にモノやサービスを売るだけでは、結局海外でも価格競争にさらされてしまうだけになることを懸念する。必要なのは、すでに述べた通り「想い」。そして、その想いが形になった姿だ。どんな国の人から見ても、その中に、美しい日本が発見できるかだ。

　ドメスティックな企業こそ、まずは自社の内なる日本らしい考え方、日本の発想、日本のアイデアを再発見、再構成し、外国人に理解しやすい形にアレン

rendering Japan itself into a brand. In the service industry, however, what is required is that concepts and "feelings" are exported having been adjusted to the local culture and ideas. Such a process, impeded by the obstacles of language and culture, has not made much ground so far.

We have finally reached a stage where the march of globalization and the advances in information and communication technology have begun to break down these barriers. We are entering an age where the high-quality Japanese "feeling" can be genuinely conveyed, an age where it is at last possible to convey this feeling if we strive hard enough. We must not confine ourselves to simply gazing in admiration at riraku's growth in the domestic market. If the earnest "feeling" of riraku can be conveyed, and if the brand can be successfully configured, growth that is many times the size of that experienced so far may well become a reality.

Companies that Grow Domestically Will Grow Worldwide

Many Japanese companies, particularly including companies focused on domestic demand, are downbeat about the gloomy outlook for the domestic their home market. Because Japanese manufacturing and services are high quality, they are often advised to – at any rate – have a go at the foreign market. This advice is not misplaced. However, my concern is that merely selling products and services will only result in becoming embroiled in price competition overseas. What is required, as I have already made clear, is "feeling." Also, that this feeling is made into a tangible form. The beauty of Japan needs to be recognizable to anybody, no matter where they are from.

Domestic companies in particular would surely benefit from a strategy of re-discovering and re-arranging the Japanese-style way of thinking and Japanese ideas that are entrenched within their company, and re-configuring them into a form that would be easily appreciated by foreign people. Expanding abroad would be plain sailing. However, the risk of being beaten at its your own game

ジして打って出る戦略が有効なのではないだろうか。ただ進出するだけならたやすい。しかし、返り討ちに遭うリスクも見逃せない。問題は、その際にブランド価値をどう上げるか、そして持続的にビジネスを行えるかなのだ。

　りらくのように、まだ国内にとどまっても、マーケットから「今後も伸びそうなビジネス」と高く評価されている企業は、すでに期待度は高い。マッチングというビジネスモデルは、国内で人材の流動化に貢献し、新たな就業機会を生み出した。お客様満足度ナンバーワンを実現するために、セラピスト満足度ナンバーワンに徹底的にこだわるからこそ、多くの人材が集まった。りらくで働いている人たちは、会社のブランドを、高い使命感とともに海外に広げていくことに人生を賭けてくれるはずだ。そして海外でも、お客様、セラピストからも信頼され、売上・利益・店舗というあらゆるビジネス指標で、大きな成功を実現するだろう。りらくには、それだけの想いと成長力、そして集う人たちの力が蓄積されている。

　りらくは、決してドメスチックな業態で終わる心配はない。これは私だけの思い込みではない。当然のように、世界に向かって日本の良さ、想いをブランドとして広げていく伝道師となっていくだろう。近い将来、マンハッタンでりらくの看板を目にする日が早く現実化することが、私には楽しみでならない。

株式会社りらく
所在地：〒595-0021
大阪府泉大津市東豊中町1丁目8番10号
設立：2010年1月8日
資本金：500万円
代表者：代表取締役社長兼CEO　出上幸典
事業内容：リラクゼーションスペースの運営

cannot be overlooked. The problem would be how to raise the brand value in such circumstances, and how to sustainably continue the business.

There are already high expectations for companies such as riraku, who while are still confined to the domestic market, which are highly evaluated by the market as businesses with high potential to grow. The business model of matching has contributed to the fluidization of domestic human resources, and has spawned new job opportunities. Many capable employees were attracted by the company's insistence on providing the highest level of satisfaction for therapists as a way to becoming the most popular company with customers. People working at riraku will no doubt dedicate their lives and feel a strong sense of mission toward taking the company brand overseas. And overseas also, they will surely enjoy enormous success in terms of all the business indices such as winning the trust of customers and therapists, sales, profits and number of stores. riraku is already bursting with the feeling and vigor required to achieve this, as well as the power of all the people it attracts.

There is no need for concern that riraku will never go beyond the domestic business category. This is not my view alone. Without doubt, riraku will evolve into an evangelist that spreads the wonder and feeling of Japan around the world. I wait with bated breath for the day when a riraku sign adorns a street corner in Manhattan. That day is surely not far off.

Company Profile:
riraku Co., Ltd.
Address: 1-8-10 Higashitoyonaka-cho, Izumiotsu-shi, Osaka 595-0021
Established: January 8, 2010
Capital: JPY 5 million
Representative: Yukinori Ideue, President/CEO
Business Description: Operation of relaxation salons.

ジャパン・ブランドの挑戦02

伝統とノウハウをブランド化して、日本の魚食文化を守りたい

ヤマセ村清　代表取締役社長
山崎祐嗣（ゆうじ）

築地のしらす最大手仲卸、ヤマセ村清。
のれんを受け継ぐ六代目経営者は、
どうブランドを構築するのか？

創業144年。消費者にはわかりにくい企業が今、
日本の食文化を支えるメインプレーヤーになろうと模索している。
どうすれば自社をブランド化できるのか、
そしてブランド化した先にどんな未来があるのか。
六代目・山崎祐嗣社長に聞いた。文中、敬称略

The Ascent of The Japan Brand 02

BRANDING TRADITION AND KNOW-HOW TO CONSERVE THE FISH CUISINE CULTURE OF JAPAN

President, YAMASE MURASEI Co., LTD.,
Yuji Yamazaki

YAMASE MURASEI, Tsukiji's largest intermediary wholesaler of *shirasu* (whitebait).
How will the sixth-generation president inheriting this reputation construct the brand?

Established 144 years ago. A company not well understood by consumers is currently seeking to become a major player in supporting Japanese food culture. How should they go about branding themselves, and what sort of future lies ahead following successful branding? I put these questions to sixth generation president Yuji Yamazaki.

築地の六代目、奮闘

午前4時。東京の台所・築地市場の朝は、外国人観光客とともに始まる。

私たちが欧米を旅行すると、たいがいは時差ボケに悩まされる。それは欧米から日本にやってきた観光客も同じだ。特に、アメリカからやってきた人たちは、未明に目が覚めてしまい、ホテルでテレビを見ながら退屈な時間を過ごすはめになりがちだ。

そんな観光客の格好のスポットになっているのが、築地市場のマグロ卸売場見学である。

「4時からマグロのせりを見学して、場外市場で寿司や海鮮丼などの朝食を取り、皇居や浅草へ向かう、というのが、近年の外国人観光客の一般的な流れのようです。とはいっても狭いところですから、なかなかゆっくり『おもてなし』ができる状況ではないんですが……」

山崎祐嗣は、世界最大ともいわれる魚市場・築地で、主に塩干物(えんかんぶつ)を扱う仲卸業、ヤマセ村清を率いる。しらすの取り扱いでは築地でトップシェア。他にも、ちりめんや煮干しといった小魚類、魚卵、干物など、全国各地の商材を取り扱っている。

その数は、2万5000点にも及ぶ。

2016年、東京都中央卸売市場は、築地から豊洲新市場への移転が予定されている。見学専用ルートの充実も図りながら、部外者と関係者の動きを切り離し、より衛生的で効率のよいマーケットを作り、日本の食文化をアピールする役割が期待されている。

「変化に適応しながら、魚食文化の豊かさを発信していきたい」

The Ascent of The Japan Brand 02 | YAMASE MURASEI Co., LTD. | Yuji Yamazaki

The Struggle of Company That Has Been in Tsukiji For Six Generations

4a.m. The morning of Tsukiji Market, Tokyo's kitchen, gets going with foreign tourists.

When we travel to Western countries, most of us are worried by jet lag. The same applies for Western tourists coming to Japan. Particularly, those travelling from America find themselves wide-awake in the early hours, cooped up in their hotel rooms watching TV.

The go-to place for such tourists is the Tsukiji Fish Market, where they can observe the wholesale tuna auctions.

"Recently, it would seem that foreign tourists tend to end up watching the tuna auctions at 4a.m., after which they eat sushi or bowls of rice topped with sashimi for breakfast just outside the market, before heading off to the Imperial Palace or Asakusa. That said, there isn't much room in here so we can't really offer them much hospitality…"

Yuji Yamazaki is the man at the helm of YAMASE MURASEI, an intermediary wholesaler dealing mainly in dried salted fish at Tsukiji, said to be the largest fish market in the world. The company commands the top share of *shirasu* at Tsukiji, as well as dealing in produce from regions all over Japan, including small varieties of fish such as *chirimen* (dried baby sardines) and *niboshi* (dried sardines,) fish roe and dried fish.

All in all, this amounts to some 25,000 items.

The Tokyo Central Wholesale Market is scheduled to move from Tsukiji to Toyosu New Market in 2016. As well as establishing a proper route specifically for spectators, it will separate outsiders from those actually working there in order to create a more hygienic and efficient market. There are high hopes that it will help promote Japan's food culture.

"I want to communicate the richness of fish food culture while adapting to change."

山崎は今、ヤマセ村清140余年の歴史を引き受けている。のれんへのこだわり、プロのまなざし。日本の水産物への誇りと、後継者の育成。そして、ブランドの構築。その取り組みは、決してやさしいものではない。

六代目経営者の奮闘を追った。

築地市場より古い歴史がある

築地に水産物・青果物の中央卸売市場が完成したのは、1935年（昭和10年）のこと。以来この場所で、80年にわたって世界最大の都市・東京の食を支え、歴史を刻んできた。

だが、ヤマセ村清のルーツは、築地市場自体よりもはるか昔までさかのぼることができる。

「日本橋の四日市にあった仲卸（なかおろし）で修業を積んでいた私の祖先が、1872年（明治5年）に独立したのが始まりです」

かつて、江戸・東京の水産物が取引されていたのは、主に日本橋だった。魚河岸は現在の日本橋三越本店の南側にあり、さらに川の対岸には、四日市と呼ばれる乾物を中心に扱う問屋街が続いていたのだという。諸説あるが、江戸時代、毎月4の日に市が立っていたことに由来するのだそうだ。

明治維新のわずか5年後。その四日市の一角で、ヤマセ村清は産声を上げた。

当初は切りイカや佃煮、さらにそれらを製造する原料を卸すビジネスを手がけていた。

1923年（大正12年）、日本橋の魚河岸は関東大震災で大打撃を受け、他の市場とともに築地へ移転することになった。四代目、山崎の祖父の時代、

The Ascent of The Japan Brand 02 | YAMASE MURASEI Co., LTD. | Yuji Yamazaki

Yamazaki has taken on YAMASE MURASEI's 140 years of history. He is committed to its reputation, and has the gaze of a professional. Proud of Japan's marine produce, he will nurture his successors. He also needs to construct the brand. These are by no means easy tasks to contend with.

I looked into the struggle faced by this sixth generation manager.

A History That Predates Tsukiji Fish Market

The central wholesale market for marine products and fruits and vegetables was established in Tsukiji in 1935 (the 10th year of the Showa Era). In the 80 years since then, it has underpinned the cuisine of Tokyo – the largest city in the world - and become imprinted upon its history.

The roots of YAMASE MURASEI, however, predate Tsukiji Market by a long way.

"It all started in 1872 (the fifth year of Meiji) when my ancestors, who learned the ropes at the intermediary wholesaler in Yokkaichi, part of Nihonbashi, went independent in 1872."

Once, Edo/Tokyo's marine products were mainly traded in Nihonbashi. The riverside fish market was located on the south side of the current Mitsukoshi Nihonbashi Main Store. On the opposite shore of the river, there was a wholesalers' district mainly dealing in dried goods, called Yokkaichi. While there are various theories, it is thought that in the Edo Period, the market took place on the fourth day of each month, hence the name "Yokkaichi" (literally "fourth day market").

A mere five years after the Meiji Restoration, YAMASE MURASEI was born in a corner of Yokkaichi.

Initially, their business revolved around the wholesale of sliced squid and fish boiled in soy sauce, as well the ingredients to make these.

The Nihonbashi riverside fish market was dealt a massive blow by the Great Kanto Earthquake of 1923 (the 12th year of Taisho) and subsequently relocated

ヤマセ村清は築地での仲卸の権利を獲得する。

終戦後は、取り扱う品数がどんどん増えていったそうだ。

「食べるモノが圧倒的に不足している時代、祖父は、困窮していた地方に対して食糧を全般的に供給するような役割を果たしていたようです。本業の塩干物だけではなく、それこそ餃子のようなものまで扱っていたといいます。当時の仲卸は、規模も、存在意義自体も本当に大きなビジネスだったようです」

そう語る山崎の横顔には、築地が置かれている苦境が見え隠れしていた。

今、築地に生きる意義

私たち一般消費者がイメージする築地は、冒頭で述べたような、マグロのせりに代表される賑やかな鮮魚取引だろう。その一方で、水産物を市場に持ち込む卸業者と、直接消費者とつながっている小売業者との間に立っている「仲卸」というビジネスがどのようなものなのかは、あまり知られていない。

山崎は、「派手なマグロに比べると、しらすなどの塩干物の仲卸は、確かに地味なんです」と笑う。しかし、しらすは単価こそ低いものの消費量が多く、

ヤマセ村清では、築地でトップシェアを誇るしらすを始め、さまざまな塩干物を取り扱っている

As well as boasting the top share of *shirasu* in Tsukiji, YAMASE MURASEI also deals in various dried-salted goods.

to Tsukiji alongside other markets. During Yamazaki's grandfather's era (the fourth generation), YAMASE MURASEI acquired the right to be an intermediary wholesaler in Tsukiji.

Following the war, he describes how they gradually increased their product lineup:

"During a time when food was in severely short supply, my grandfather apparently took up the role of providing general foodstuffs to regions that were in extreme difficulty. As well as his main business of dried salted foods, he dealt in a whole range of foods, which even included gyoza dumplings. It appears that to be an intermediary wholesaler at the time was genuinely a major business, both in terms of scale and also in terms of significance of existence."

As Yamazaki explains this, his facial expression cannot quite conceal the difficulties that Tsukiji is facing today.

What is Means to Be in Tsukiji Today

General consumers like you and I tend to perceive Tsukiji as a bustling place where fresh fish is traded, typified by tuna auctions, as I described above. In contrast, not much is known about the business called "intermediary wholesaler," which stand in-between the wholesalers that bring marine products into the market and the retailers who directly serve consumers.

Yamazaki jests: "Compared to gorgeous tuna, intermediary wholesale of dried salted fish like *shirasu* is definitely somewhat unspectacular." While the actual unit cost for *shirasu* is low, the amount consumed is high; when seen in terms of monetary amounts, in Tsukiji it is only second to tuna for transaction volume. It is also the category of fish that commands the leading position for pricing in Tsukiji Market. "At auctions, you don't get the flamboyant shouting you hear with tuna. Our battle is a make-or-break game where bids are made by prices written on a piece of paper. It is real psychological warfare."

Using pricing trends up until the previous day as a benchmark, and while

金額ベースで見れば、築地ではマグロに次ぐ取扱量を誇っている。そして、今でも築地市場がプライシングの主導権を握っている魚種なのだという。
「せりでは、マグロのような派手な掛け声はありません。僕たちの戦いは、主に紙に書いた価格で入札する一発勝負。これはこれで、なかなかの心理戦なんですよ」
前日までの価格推移をベースに、天候の変化や今後のマーケットの需給といった複雑なファクターに頭を巡らせながら、モノとしての良し悪しを総合的に判断して入札価格を決める。水産物の専門家としての鑑識眼だけでなく、市場参加者としての相場観、ライバルに対しての勝負強さも求められる。
はためには、なかなか面白そうなビジネスに見える。しかし、山崎の表情は穏やかではない。
「置かれている状況は、大変厳しい。自分たちの存在意義を、今後どう見出すのか。変わっていく世界の中で、充実感と無力感との狭間に立っているというのが、正直な今の状況なのです」
築地では、同業他社の廃業が目立っているという。
マグロをはじめ鮮魚関連の仲卸の業況は決して悪くない。品質に応じて適正な価格がつきやすく、築地の顔として機能している。ただ、ヤマセ村清の扱う塩干物は、質が良くても、高い価格は敬遠される傾向にある。次第に市場外流通も多くなってきている。
「本当は面白い世界なんです。でも、伝わらないのが悔しい」

目利きたちの「眼」は何を見ている?

塩干物のスタートは、そもそも「保存」のためだった。現在のような物流体

internally processing complicated factors such as changes in weather and future market supply and demand, they determines the bidding price by making a comprehensive judgment on the merits and demerits of the produce in question.

More than just having the critical eye of an expert, each bidder needs to have an outlook on the market price as a market participant and the ability to compete with their rivals. From the outside, it does look like an interesting business. However, Yamazaki's expression is not so serene.

"We are facing seriously tough times. Discovering our future raison d'etre is a serious question. In all honesty, in a changing world we find ourselves sandwiched between a sense of accomplishment and a sense of helplessness."

In Tsukiji, there is a palpable sense of rivals going out of business.

The state of the industry for fresh fish-related intermediary wholesalers – including tuna - is certainly not bad. Tuna fetches an adequate price in line with quality, and functions as the face of Tsukiji. Nevertheless, despite their high quality, YAMASE MURASEI's dried salted marine products tend to be given the cold shoulder due to their high price. Off-market distribution is also gradually on the rise.

"It really is an interesting world. However, it pains me that it falls on deaf ears."

しらすのせりは、入札者が落札価格を記入した紙をせり人に渡すと、すぐ落札者が決まる

At a *shirasu* auction, once bidders pass a piece of paper with their bid price to the auctioneer, the winning bidder is swiftly decided.

制がない時代、海が遠く、鮮魚を口にできない地方に住む人たちは、魚を塩干物として摂取していた。

たとえば、アジの開き一枚にしても、原料を吟味し、仕入れ、加工し、運搬する手間がかかる。それぞれにプロの技があるのだが、鮮魚が全国どこでも入手可能になった現代の日本では、なかなかそこに価値を見出してもらいにくい。

「干物は安いモノだという思い込みが残り、ちょっとした手間賃も嫌われてしまう」。山崎はくやしがる。

だが、よく話を聞いていくと、山崎の話は実に興味深い。知らなかった知識が次々に得られ、奥深さに感銘を受ける。

「小女子のおいしい時期って、ご存じですか?」

小女子なんて、年中同じだと思っていた。

「小女子は、イカナゴという魚の稚魚です。限られた湾内でしか獲れない魚で、漁期は3月〜5月のはしり(初め)だけ。暑くなると砂に潜って獲れなくなりますから、この時期に1年分を冷凍して、安定供給します。だから春先しか食べられないフレッシュな味があります」

ヤマセ村清のメインであるしらすは、東北南部から鹿児島までの太平洋岸を中心に広い範囲で獲れる。こちらは漁期が長く、獲れない時期は数ヵ月間だけ。旬の時期を感じにくい。

「ただ、私たちにはモノの良し悪しはすぐわかります。サイズや色などの特性、季節による味の変化などによって、独自に分けています。一度も冷凍していないしらすはびっくりするほどおいしいんです」

しらすとセットで食べられることの多い大根おろし。実は「缶詰のシロップ」のようなモノなのだという。流通の過程で飛んだしらすの潤いを補い、のどごし

What Do the Connoisseur's Eyes See?

"*Enkanbutsu*" (salted dried marine products) started from the need for preservation. In an era without the distribution systems of today, people in regions far from the sea were unable to access fresh fish, and consumed fish in a salted, dried form.

For example, even a simple *aji no hiraki* (cut open and dried horse mackerel) requires a lot of time an effort, involving carefully selecting the raw product, procurement, processing and transport. Despite each of these requiring professional skill, it is hard to convey the value of this in the Japan of today where fresh fish can be obtained anywhere across the country.

"People are still under the impression that dried foods are cheap; they are loath to pay a little charge for the labor involved." Yamazaki feels chagrined.

As Yamazaki continues, I realize that his story is genuinely fascinating. I learn a great deal of new things, and am deeply impressed by the depth of his knowledge.

"Do you know the time of year when young lancefish are most tasty?"

I assumed that young lancefish were the same throughout the year.

"Young lancefish are the juvenile fish of the Japanese sand lance. Only a limited number can be caught inside the bay, and only between March and early May. Once it gets warm they descend into the sand and can no longer be fished. So, during this period you freeze one year's worth to ensure a steady supply. That is why they only taste fresh around the beginning of spring."

Shirasu, YAMASE MURASEI's mainstay product, are fished over a wide range centering on the Pacific coast from Southern Tohoku all the way to Kagoshima. The fishing season is long, with only a few months when fish cannot be caught. It is hard to sense when they are in season.

"We can quickly distinguish what is good and what is not. We have our own way of dividing them up, according to characteristic like size and color, as well as the change in taste due to the seasons. *Shirasu* that have not been frozen at

を良くするためのモノなのだそうだ。

「本当においしいしらすは、醤油なしでいけます。しかし、そこまで良いモノの流通量は、ごくわずかです」

未経験のおいしさを消費者にどう伝えられるか

興味深いエピソードを聞いた。

山崎の子どもは、山崎が自信を持って人に薦められる高級しらすを持ち帰って食卓に出すと、眼を丸くして、一心不乱に食べる。ところが、もったいないからと引き取ってきたしらすは、「今日のはおいしくない!」と言って残すというのだ。

さすが、長年しらすを扱う家業の家に生まれた子どもだ。「まだ何も知らないだけに、正直です」と山崎は笑う。

だが、私はここに新しい可能性を感じる。

以前の私を含め、ほとんどの消費者は、しらすが嫌いではないにもかかわらず、本当においしい、一度も冷凍していない釜揚げしらすやしらす干しを口にした経験がないだけなのではないのか。騙されたと思って食べてみるといい。本当においしい。

いかに私たちが高度な流通の行き届いた社会を、それだけに誰の手を経てどのように届いたかわからないモノを口にする社会を生きていようと、山崎の子どものように、おいしいモノとそうではないモノの区別は、直感的にできる。

ところが、ことしらすに関しては、まだ漁港に出向いて食べる人は少数派だ。多くの消費者がスーパーで何となく買い求め、深く考えずに残った分を冷凍庫にしまう。

all are surprisingly delicious."

Shirasu are often served with grated *daikon* (white radish). He explains that actually the daikon functions rather like the syrup in canned food. It replenishes the moisture in the fish that is lost in the distribution process, making them slip down the throat well.

"With really delicious *shirasu*, you don't even need soy sauce. However, *shirasu* of this quality are only available in tiny quantities."

The Challenge of Conveying to Consumers an Undiscovered Sumptuous Taste

Yamazaki shared an interesting episode with me.

When Yamazaki brings home high-grade *shirasu* that he can recommend to people with confidence and places it on the dinner table, his children's eyes widen and they devour it wholeheartedly. Conversely, if he brings home *shirasu* that was otherwise going to be discarded and wasted, they turn their noses up at it and leave it on the plate, exclaiming that "it is not delicious at all!"

Exactly what you might expect of children who grew up in the house of a long-running *Shirasu* merchant. Yamazaki chuckles: "They don't know the whole picture yet, but are at least honest."

I, however, sensed a new possibility in this.

While most consumers - up until now myself included - do not actively dislike *shirasu*, they have probably never experienced really delicious non-frozen *shirasu* that have been cooked in a pot, or the equally sumptuous dried *shirasu*. People really need to find out just how delicious the real thing is.

Despite the fact that we live in a society with extremely advanced distribution systems where we have no idea who was responsible for delivering the food that arrives on our plates, like Yamazaki's children, we are capable of intuitively distinguishing between that which is delicious and that which is not.

With regard to *shirasu* in particular, there are hardly any people who have yet made the journey to a fishing harbor to eat them. Most consumers just buy them

「なぜそうするのか。そうすることによって質がどうなるのか」を一切考えないまま、しらすなんてこの程度のモノではないか、と勝手に思い込んでいる。

　でも本当は、真においしいモノを、しかるべき人から「おいしい理由」を教えてもらい、美しい環境の中で食べれば、単なる食事を超えた、一層豊かな経験にできる。ここに、ヤマセ村清の挑戦のヒントが隠されているように思えてならない。

　目利きによるレコメンド。歴史と文化を感じることのできるバックグラウンドヒストリーが合わされば、顧客がむしろ喜んでお金を払いたくなるようなブランドが築けるはずなのだ。

ノウハウはブランドにできる

　たとえば、山崎はこんなことも教えてくれる。
「しらすは、なかなか難しい食材なんです。そもそも一口にしらすと言ってもいろいろな魚種の稚魚の総称ですから。私たちの知識と眼なら、肌ツヤ、色との全体のバランス、獲れた時期などによって、ある程度見分けはつく。ただ農産物とは違って、ある時期にある漁港に揚がったしらすを、有名な業者が釜揚げした商品だからといっても、魚種やタイミングによってまったく質が変わってくる。生の場合は、獲れてからの時間と衛生的なレベルの確認との見合いもある。難しいし、面白い食材です」

　こうしたヤマセ村清のノウハウそのものを、ブランドにできないだろうか。私は、挑戦の第一歩はそこから始まるように思える。

　ヤマセ村清はあくまで仲卸だから、自社商品はない。でも、しらすを知り尽くしたヤマセ村清だからこそ、自信を持ってセレクトしたしらすを顧客に薦められる。

in the supermarket, and freeze any leftovers without giving it too much thought.

Most people just assume that this is what *shirasu* taste like, without giving any thought whatsoever to why they freeze them or how this affects the quality.

Actually, if a competent person could show them the real taste and explain "the reason why they taste so good" - if they could only eat *shirasu* in beautiful surroundings in a restaurant that serves them properly, they would have a truly delicious experience that goes above and beyond a mere meal. I cannot help feeling that this offers a hint for how YAMASE MURASEI can rise to the challenge.

A recommendation by a connoisseur. A chance to understand the history, culture and background of the food. With these elements present, it should be possible to create a brand for which customers would be happy to open their wallets for.

Know-how Can Make the Brand

For instance, Yamazaki also shared with me the following:
"*Shirasu* is actually quite a tricky ingredient. The word *shirasu* is basically a catch-all for various kinds of juvenile fish. If you have our eyes and knowledge, you can to an extent distinguish between them based on the glow of their skin, overall balance with color, and the time of year at which they were caught. However, in contrast to agricultural produce, the quality of *shirasu* differs enormously depending on the variety of fish and timing, even if it is a product that was caught at a certain time and in a certain fishing harbor, and then cooked in an iron pot by a famous trader. If eaten raw, you have to counterbalance a certain level of hygiene with waiting a certain amount of time after landing them. It is a tricky, but fascinating ingredient."

Could this know-how of YAMASE MURASEI not be encapsulated into a brand, I wonder. I get the feeling that this constitutes the first step of their challenge.

YAMASE MURASEI is after all a wholesaler that does not have its own company products. That said, it is precisely YAMASE MURASEI with its

目利きの力そのものを、ブランドに変えていけるはずだ。

　超高級品から普及品にいたるまで、価格の背景を知識や文化とともに説明し、顧客の納得感を高めた上で購入してもらう。もちろん、パッケージにはレコメンダーとしてのプライドをかけて、ヤマセ村清のマークが輝く。
「今後、自分たちで吟味したものを販売したり、自分たちが加工場までコミットして、品質にこだわった塩干物を販売したりしてみたい。上から下まで扱うビジネスはもちろん、納得の上で売りたい」
　OEMのような展開だけでなく、究極のしらす丼やこだわりの干物を出すアンテナショップが展開されても面白いだろう。
　もし、醤油すらかけるのをためらうようなしらす丼が食べられる店を、築地最大手、創業140年の老舗が手がけたら？　私なら、1500円でも食べてみたいと思う。そこで殴られるような感動を覚えれば、今度は友人を誘う。
　ブランド再構築の基礎になるのは、ヤマセ村清の看板と、そこに集う人の眼なのだ。

日本から台湾へ、台湾から世界へ

　ヤマセ村清を支えているもうひとつのキーワードは、輸出だ。
　国内事業と並行し、30年ほど前から子会社を通じて台湾への輸出を手がけている。そのきっかけは、人と人との縁だった。
「ビジネス抜き、たまたまのご縁で紹介されたのが、現在の台湾側パートナー企業、富帆貿易の創業者だったのです」
　当初はヤマセ村清が富帆側から商品を買う形で取引が始まった。
　ところが、富帆が日本の食品を売りたいと考え、ヤマセ村清が日本で調達し

extensive knowledge of *shirasu* that is in a position to confidently recommend carefully selected *shirasu* to its customers. It should be possible to imbue the connoisseur capabilities into a brand.

From ultra luxury goods to popular goods, explain to customers the background to pricing along with elements of knowledge and culture, till they are convinced about making a purchase. Of course, the package would be adorned with the YAMASE MURASEI mark as a sign of proud endorsement.
"Looking ahead, we would love to sell fish that we have carefully scrutinized, and commit to having a processing factory in order to sell dried salted goods of the highest quality. We would of course love to run a top-to-bottom selling business once we are convinced of its feasibility."

As well as leveraging OEM, it would also be great to see development of antenna shops serving the ultimate *shirasu* rice-bowl dishes and other handpicked dried foods.

How about if an industry-leading shop in Tsukuji established for 140 years opened a restaurant where you could eat a *shirasu* rice bowl that is so good that you would hesitate to even put soy sauce on? I would definitely pay 1,500 yen for the privilege. If I were to be bowled over by the taste, I would invite my friends the next time. The key to reconstructing the brand lies in YAMASE MURASEI's signboards and the discerning eyes of the people who gather there.

Japan to Taiwan, Taiwan to the World

Another keyword underpinning YAMASE MURASEI is 'export.'

In parallel to its domestic business, they started exporting to Taiwan some 30 years ago through subsidiary companies. The catalyst for this was actually a fortuitous and auspicious encounter.

"Rather than business, it was a chance encounter with the founder of Huhan Trading, our current partner in Taiwan."

Initially, the business relationship started out with YAMASE MURASEI

た食品を冷凍で台湾に送り、台湾で富帆が商社として販売するビジネスが出来上がった。水産物だけでなく、みそ、醤油、みりんなどの調味料や、加工食品など、より一般的な日本産の食品も多く扱っている。

　台湾は歴史的経緯からもあってもともと親日的で、日本食へのニーズが高かっただけでなく、日本の小売、外食企業の進出によって一段と需要が増えている。富帆貿易は、台湾の大手商社兼食品問屋にまで成長した。食材の輸入、冷蔵・冷凍温度帯を備えた自社倉庫での保管から、1日3回ものデリバリーまでを一貫して展開し、現地企業、日系企業ともに厚い信頼を得ている。

　さらに、早い時期に日台間の冷凍流通ルートを開拓できたおかげで、ヤマセ村清には、他社からルートを使わせてほしいという引き合いも増えている。
「どこにご縁や商売のきっかけが隠されているのか、わからないものですね」
　輸出の伸長は、成長の大きな原動力になると山崎は確信している。当面は台湾企業との協力関係を足がかりに、多方面への展開を検討している。
「アジアだけでなく、魚食文化、健康食ブームが広がっている欧米を含めて、今後どう展開していこうか思案しているところです」

日本クオリティの「功罪」

　海外における寿司をはじめとした和食文化の普及はめざましく、日本人としては少しうれしいところだが、一方で豊かな外国人が魚を食べるようになったことで、必ずしも日本人の消費者には有利にはならない状況も起きているという。
「近年、明らかに魚価が上がっています」
　今まで、日本人にとって魚は安くて当たり前のタンパク源だった。世界中から魚を集められて、食べる国が少なかったのだから。

purchasing products from Huhan.

However, Huhan wanted to sell Japanese products, so YAMASE MURASEI froze food products procured in Japan and sent them to Taiwan. This marked the start of Huhan's business as a trading company selling to Taiwanese customers. As well as marine products, they also deal in more general Japanese food products, including processed foods, and seasonings such as *miso*, soy sauce and *mirin* (sweet cooking rice wine).

Taiwan has historically been pro-Japan, and in addition to significant needs for Japanese food, the advance of Japanese retail and restaurant businesses have raised demand yet further. Huhan has grown into one of Taiwan's largest trading companies and food wholesale merchants. Foodstuffs are imported and kept in their own company storehouse that has a cold storage and refrigerated temperature zone. From there it makes three deliveries every day to local companies and Japanese-affiliated companies, from whom they enjoy loyal patronage.

Furthermore, thanks to having cultivated a frozen distribution route between Taiwan and Japan from an early stage, YAMASE MURASEI is increasingly approached by other companies who want to make use of this route.
"You never know where a new relationship or business chance will spring from."

Yamazaki is convinced that the growth in exports will be a major driving force for growth. In the meantime, the cooperative relationships with Taiwanese companies will be a foothold for considering expansion into many other fields.
"We are currently deliberating how to expand in future, not just in Asia, but also in Western countries which are undergoing a boom in fish food culture and healthy foods."

The Merits and Demerits of Japanese Quality

Sushi and other elements of Japanese food culture are becoming remarkably

だが、状況は次第に変わりつつある。

「ここ10〜15年ほどで、海外マーケットに対する買い負けはかなり進んでいます。その上、一等級がなかなか築地に来にくくなっているのです」

築地市場の象徴といえるマグロは、何とか集散拠点としての地位を保っているが、たとえばホタテなどの他の鮮魚に関しては、産地で加工された後、そのまま中国や欧米に流れることが当たり前になった。買い付ける量も、投じられる金額もまるで異なるのだから、産地としては当然有利になる取引を選ぶ。

これは、食の質、そして安全性に高いこだわりとクオリティを持つ日本のブランドが信頼されている結果でもあるという。少々皮肉な話でもある。

築地で朝取引された鮮魚が、同じ日の夕方には香港のレストランに並ぶ時代。本当においしいモノ、信頼できるモノをめぐるビジネスは、「奪い合い」とも言える状況を呈しているのだ。

日本の消費者の立場とすれば、不安を覚えてしまう。しかし、日本の水産物を高く買ってもらえること自体は、ヤマセ村清のような企業には有利に働く。

「ビジネスチャンスを広げるだけでなく、和食文化の海外普及の両面から貢献していく方法を模索しています」

攻める人材はこう育てる

人にこそ蓄積される目利きの能力。そして広がる輸出業の可能性。今後のヤマセ村清を支えていくのは、若い力だ。

「当社はまだまだ少数精鋭ですから、ひとりの比重は大変大きい。一人前になるまでに時間もかかります。ところがありがたいことに、最近はリニューアルしたホームページを見て、自ら応募してくれる若い人も現れています」

popular overbroad. While this is a welcome development for Japanese people, wealthy foreigners developing a taste for eating fish could spell trouble for Japanese consumers.

"Recently, the price of fish is definitely going up."

Up until now, fish was a cheap source of protein that was taken for granted. It was possible to import fish from all over the world, as not many countries favored it.

However, the situation is gradually changing.

"In the last 10 -15 years, we are increasingly losing out on purchases to foreign markets. On top of that, top grade fish increasingly does not make it into Tsukiji Market."

Tsukiji still remains the hub for tuna distribution, which has become a byword for the market. However, these days it has become the norm for other fresh fish such as scallops to be processed where they are landed and then sent off straight to China or Western countries. Foreign buyers want higher quantity and are prepared to pay a higher price; it is no surprise that producers opt for the more advantageous offers.

This is also a result of the fact that Japanese brands are highly trusted for the quality of food and high insistence on safety. It is all somewhat ironic.

We are now in an era where fresh fish traded in the morning at Tsukiji is already adorning plates on restaurants in Hong Kong by the evening. The business of obtaining really delicious and reliable food has brought about a situation that could be described as "a scramble."

Seen from the perspective of the Japanese consumer, this is cause for concern. That said, the fact that Japanese marine produce can be sold for a high price is something that a company such as YAMASE MURASEI can use to their advantage.

"As well as expanding business chances, we are exploring ways to kill two birds with one stone by also contributing to the spread of *Washoku* (Japanese cuisine) culture overseas."

心強い話だ。山崎がそんな若い人たちと接して感じたことを、こう分析する。まず、築地が一種のブランドとして機能することで、「築地で働いてみたい」という思いを持つ人が増えた。もうひとつは、築地で長年続いている企業が持っているはずの、プロ集団としての「本物感」に魅力を感じていることだ。
「ありがたい話です。特殊な世界ですから、志を同じくする人を、じっくり育てていきたいと考えています」
　水産物の知識、業界の決まりごと、独特の人間関係だけでなく、マーケット参加者としての感覚までを身につけてもらうには、最低でも6〜8年はかかるという。そして、そこに便利な育成マニュアルはない。
「50代のベテランと一緒に仕事をしてもらい、彼らが引退する頃に何とか一人前になってほしい」
　山崎が期待しているのは、決してこれまでと同じ人材の再生産ではない。伝統を引き継ぎながら、新しいフィールドを自ら開いてくれる人材に育てなければ意味がない。
「価格競争に巻き込まれるような状況に甘んじるわけにはいきません。そのためには、従来型の『待ち』一辺倒の仲卸から、どう自分で仕掛けて商売を作

しらすは築地でマグロに次ぐ取扱量を誇る
After tuna, *shirasu* boasts the second largest transaction volume in Tsukiji.

This is How to Nurture Proactive Self-Starting Employees

The ability to discern, built up in people slowly over time. The increasing potential for export business. The power to sustain YAMASE MURASEI into the future will come from the young generation.

"Our company is still just a select few, so the weight on each individual is considerable. It takes time before they can stand on their own two feet. However, thankfully, recently there are youngsters who apply to us having seen our homepage that we revamped."

It is a reassuring tale. The following is an analysis of what Yamazaki feels having come into contact with such youngsters. First of all, through Tsukiji functioning as a brand of sorts, an increasing number of youngsters feel that they would like to work there. They also feel the lure of a group of professionals that is the "genuine article," a company that is a veritable part of the woodwork of Tsukiji.

"It is a most promising sign. This is a specialized world, so we would like to take the time to properly educate and nurture people who share the same vision."

In addition to teaching the know-how of marine produce, the ways of the industry and the unique inter-personal relationships, to imbue in someone the perception required to be a market participant takes a minimum of six to eight years. No helpful education manual exists for this purpose.

"I'll have them work alongside veterans in their 50s, in the hope that they'll be able to stand on their own two feet by the time those veterans retire."

Yamazaki is certainly not expecting to reproduce the same personnel that existed up until now. It is meaningless unless new recruits can be handed over traditions while at the same time taking the initiative in cultivating new fields themselves.

"It would not do to settle for being caught up in a price competition. To prevail from now on, it will be important to evolve from being an intermediary

り出せるようになれるかが勝負です」

 山崎自身も、社長業、トップ営業の傍ら、人材の育成と組織作りに自ら注力する。

「若い連中には、この世界、このビジネスが持っている、面白くて広い世界を見せてやりたい」

ブランド力は「発信力」

「待ち」一辺倒の仲卸からの脱却。山崎の強い決意を支えるものは、まさにブランドだ。そして、山崎が心配している以上に、ヤマセ村清にはすでにブランドの萌芽がたくさん宿っているように見える。

 老舗としての本物の歴史。変わりゆく時代を生き抜き、業態を変えながら社会と食文化に貢献してきた事実。そして、長年の経験によって今もプロ集団の中に息づいている目利きとしての能力と、蓄積された知識、ノウハウ。ヤマセ村清にもし不足しているものがあるとすれば、それは「発信する力」なのではないだろうか。

 どうすれば、ヤマセ村清の想い、考え方やモノの見方、そしてそれらを統合するブランドが人々に届くのだろうか。すでにある本物のブランドを、しっかりブランディングすることができるのだろうか。最初のキーワードは「視覚化」だ。

 高品質を見抜く力、経験。それらはすばらしい財産である一方で、他者からはその度合いが見えにくい。

 しかし世界には、ヤマセ村清のような本物の企業が、いくらでもブランディングに成功し、飛躍している例がある。まずは、ヤマセ村清の歴史と力を「見える形」に落とし込むことだ。自社ブランドを押し出し、ヤマセ村清がおいしいと

wholesaler exclusively devoted to the conventional 'passive waiting for orders' to a company that can take the initiative in cultivating new business itself."

Yamazaki himself, as well as being company president and handling sales at the top level, will put all his resources into nurturing talented employees and building the organization.

"I want to show youngsters the fascinating and varied world that this business offers."

Brand Power is All About Communicability

Moving away from being an intermediary wholesaler devoted to "waiting." Underpinning Yamazaki's strong resolve is quite simply, having a brand. On this front, it would appear that despite Yamazaki's concerns, there are already many budding sprouts of a brand present within YAMASE MURASEI.
The proud history of a longstanding intermediary wholesaler. The fact that they have lived throughout changing generations and adapted their business with the aim of contributing to both food culture and society. On top of this, connoisseurship that is alive and well within a group of professionals thanks to many years of experience, their accumulated knowledge and expertise. If there is anything that could be said to be lacking within YAMASE MURASEI, it would probably be the "ability to reach out."

How can YAMASE MURASEI ensure that their ideas and perspectives, together with the brand that unites them, actually reach people? Will they be able to re-brand an already well-established brand? The first keyword is "visualization."

The ability and experience to detect high quality. While this is a tremendous asset, it is difficult for others to see it to the full extent.

In the world, however, there are examples of "genuine article" corporations of YAMASE MURASEI's ilk who have successfully created a brand and are making great leaps forward. The most pressing task is to "render into visible

いうモノなら信頼できる、という流れを生み出せるといい。

　もうひとつは、食文化が持つ圧倒的な「おいしさ」を、有無を言わせず味わわせることだ。高くてもいい。雨が続いて良い品が入らないなら臨時休業してもいい。ただ、ヤマセ村清の出すしらす丼なら絶対に間違いがない、というブランド感は出せるはずだ。

　大手流通にはできないことをひたすら追求してほしい。一流の器で、獲った人、加工した人、調理した人のこだわりと、おいしさの背景をあますところなく説明すれば、誰もが納得できる。その完璧感こそ、ヤマセ村清のまたとないブランドになるはずだ。

伝統を受け継ぐ者として

　六代目のプレッシャー。そこには、相当な重圧があるはずだ。経営に当たって、自分の意志だけに素直になれるものなのだろうか。
「私は大卒後すぐに入社しました。父の背中を見て、父の教えを請いながら修業していたのですが、途中で父は亡くなってしまった。それからは、社員や周囲のお取引先に面倒を見てもらいながらここまでどうにかやってきました」
　山崎は謙虚だった。もし新卒後の数年を、他社、それも他業界での修業に費やしていたら、先代の急死できっと何もできなかっただろうという。
「築地はマーケットですから、ある意味シビアな世界でもあります。創業144年だ、六代目だなんて、ここではたいして古くもありませんしね」
　マグロの仲卸には、江戸時代から十数代続いている業者もある。それぞれに後継者問題は抱えつつも、もし撤退しそうなところがあれば、そのシェアを奪いに来るしたたかさも決して隠さない。

form" the history and prowess of YAMASE MURASEI. A good outcome would be to push out their own company brand, leading to a situation where "if YAMASE MURASEI says it is good, you can take their word for it."

Another task would be to have consumers experience willy-nilly the overwhelming "deliciousness" inherent in their food culture. It does not matter if this is expensive. It also does not matter if the store shuts temporarily when heavy rain prevents them from obtaining good quality produce. Simply, it should be possible to ferment the brand feeling that the *shirasu* rice bowl that YAMASE MURASEI serves is the very best that there is.

I hope that they patiently pursue something that is beyond the abilities of major distributors. If served on elegant tableware, along with an exhaustive explanation of the obsessiveness of the people who caught, processed and prepared the fish, together with the background to why it is so delicious, anybody would be convinced. It is precisely this sense of perfection that will create YAMASE MURASEI's once-in-a-lifetime brand.

An Heir to Tradition

The pressure of the sixth generation. This must be a heavy burden. When it comes to management, is he able to simply act on his own volition?
"I entered the company straight after graduating university. I looked towards my father and trained up while requesting his guidance. However, my father passed away in the midst of this process. Since then, I somehow managed to make my way to where I am today under the guidance of other employees and business partners."

Yamazaki's reaction was modest. Had he invested several years since graduating in another company or indeed training in another industry, he would never have been able to step into his father's shoes.
"Because Tsukiji is a market, it is a demanding place in certain aspects. Here, 144 years of operations and six generations of owners, is not particularly old."

その中で生き抜いてきたヤマセ村清には、山崎に受け継がれている謙虚さが代々伝わっていた。マーケット感覚が高じて株式や不動産の取引に手を出すようなこともなかった。
「自分たちが謙虚だとか、歴史が長い、伝統企業だなどと思うのはまったくの奢りで、それだけ長い歴史の中で、多くのお客様やお取引先と触れ合いながら続いてきた感謝があるだけなのです。ただ最近は、感謝だけではいけないと感じています。周囲の方に褒めていただける以上は、私たちの内側に、何か誇れるもの、ブランド化できるモノが本当はもっと隠されているのではないか、という気づきです。まだ、この築地の仲卸では少数派かもしれません」
　いわば、今の築地、今の日本を生きている企業が持つ、ミッション。
　山崎が感じ取っている変化とは、どんなものなのだろうか。

魚食文化への貢献

　山崎には、自社ののれんの重み以上に、大切にしたいことがある。それは、日本の魚食文化そのものだ。
「和食、と言ってしまうとちょっと張り切り過ぎかもしれません。魚食文化でも大げさならば、素材でもいい。魚を食べるという文化、そしてその文化を支える水産業が強くなっていくにはどうすればいいのか」
　私なりに山崎を応援すると、逆に、他の人がしようとしないことだからこそ、挑戦する価値が高いように思えてならない。
　挑戦しない人には、それなりの理由があるのだろう。自分たちには荷が重いとか、出過ぎた真似だと考えているのかもしれない。
　ただ私が、あくまで一消費者としてどうすれば山崎のミッション達成ができる

With intermediary wholesalers of tuna, there are merchants who have been going for ten or more generations since the Edo Era. While they all have respective difficulties in finding successors, if they see someone about to pull out from the business, they won't be afraid to usurp that share.

In a YAMASE MURASEI that has lived throughout these times, the modesty handed down to Yamazaki has spanned the generations. They have not sought to develop their keen sense of the market into other businesses, such as those related to the stock market or real estate.

"To say that we are modest, or that our history is long or that we are a traditional corporation is nothing but pride. We are simply grateful for the fact that over the years we have been sustained by interacting with customers and business partners. Recently, however, I do feel that being grateful is not enough to sustain us. Thanks to receiving praise and encouragement from people around us, I have realized that we have something concealed inside that is actually something we can be proud of, something that we can render into a brand. We are still in the minority as a intermediary wholesaler in this Tsujkiji Market."

The mission, so to speak, held by corporations in Japan and in Tsukiji today. What exactly is the change that Yamazaki is picking up on?

Contributing to the Culture of Fish Food

Beyond the weight of his company's reputation, there is something else Yamazaki highly values. That is, Japan's fish food culture itself.

"It might be a bit of a stretch to say *Washoku*. If fish food culture is also a bit over the top, then ingredients will suffice. What needs to be done to ensure that the culture of eating fish and the marine produce industry that sustains it becomes stronger?"

I really feel like supporting Yamazaki precisely because he is trying to do what nobody else is, and the challenge that he is pursuing is of immense value.

かを考えれば、むしろ仲卸のような立場の企業、人こそ、文化としての魚食、産業としての水産、そして世界に誇れるジャパン・ブランドとしての日本の食文化を支えられる立場にいるのではないかと思えてならない。

　生産者にも、加工者にも、消費者にも——。そして海外にもフットワーク軽く踏み込んでいく。そのためには仲卸がブランド化したほうがいいし、魚食文化の中心にいてハブの役割を果たしていることこそ、すべてが効率だけで動き過ぎている現代の食生活から、本当に良いモノへのリスペクトとリーズナブルな価格設定という解を導く貢献ができるはずだ。

「流れに乗ること、流れの中で自分たちなりにアレンジしていくことを意識できなければ、結局流れに飲み込まれるだけになってしまう。ずっと同じことをやっていたら、ヤマセ村清はそもそも今まで続いていないはずです。変化を恐れず、より一層、深く深く追い求めていきたい」

　誰もやらないからこそ、そこにチャンスがある。私もそう信じている。

株式会社ヤマセ村清
所在地：〒104－0045　東京都中央区築地6-26-7宮崎ビル　5F
設立：明治5年（1872年）
資本金：1000万円
代表者：代表取締役社長　山崎祐嗣
事業内容：しらす干し等（塩干小魚）、魚卵、干物各種、海産珍味、冷凍魚各種、その他

Those who do not seek to rise to the challenge must surely have good reasons for it. They might feel that the burden is too great for them or that they need to remember their place, not to get ideas above their station.

As a general consumer, when I think about what Yamazaki has to do in order to achieve his mission, I cannot help but think that it is exactly somebody in the position of intermediary wholesaler who is best poised to sustain the culture of eating fish, the fishing industry and the Japan Brand representing the nation's food culture that can be the pride of the world

For producers, for processors, for consumers alike....And, quick legwork to expand overseas. For these reasons it is worthwhile for an intermediary wholesaler to from their own brand; indeed, precisely because of their role as a hub at the center of fish food culture, they are in a good position to educate consumers about having respect for genuinely delicious foods alongside reasonable price setting, moving away from existing eating habits which are too fast-moving and revolve exclusively around efficiency.

"If you don't tap into the flow or are not aware of arranging things your own way within the flow, you will simply end up being swallowed up by the flow. YAMASE MURASEI, by all rights, should not have made it this far by always doing the same thing. Not fearing change, we want to passionately pursue our goals at an even deeper level than ever before."

If nobody else is doing it, therein lies opportunity. This is what I believe.

Company Profile:
YAMASE MURASEI Co., LTD.
Address: 5F Miyazaki Bldg. 6-26-7 Tsukiji, Chuo-ku, Tokyo 104-0045
Established: 1872
Capital: JPY 10 million
Representative: Yuji Yamazaki, President
Business Description:
Wholesale of dried whitebait (dried-salted small fish),
fish roe, and various dried/frozen and processed fish products/delicacies.

ジャパン・ブランドの挑戦03

教習所が
ディズニーランドを
超える日

武蔵境自動車教習所　代表取締役会長
髙橋 勇

教習所になぜ花火は上がるのか？
社員の力を引き出す「おもてなし経営」の秘密

日本のモータリゼーションとともに成長してきた自動車教習所。
少子高齢化と都市部のクルマ離れで6割の顧客が消え、
今では多くが苦境に立たされている。
その中で、確固たる理念をもとに現在もなお成長を続けている
「東京車人」武蔵境自動車教習所。その内側を探った。文中、敬称略

The Ascent of The Japan Brand 03

THE DAY A DRIVING SCHOOL SURPASSES DISNEYLAND

Chairman, Musashisakai Driving School Co., LTD.
Isamu Takahashi

Why are there fireworks at a driving school? The secret of "hospitable management" to draw out employee's capabilities

Driving schools grew alongside Japan's motorization. The number of customers has fallen by 60percent of due to the falling birth rate and aging population, as well as urbanites not wanting to get behind the wheel, leaving the industry in a painful predicament. In such circumstances, "Tokyo Shajin" Musashisakai Driving School has continued to grow based on its rock steady ideology. I took a look inside.

98％が満足し、新しい顧客を連れてくる教習所

　成長を続け、まさに今、業績のピークを叩き出している自動車教習所が東京都内にある、と聞いたら、私なら耳を疑う。直感的に、そんなはずはないと考えてしまうからだ。

　少子化と若年層のクルマ離れは著しい。特にクルマがなくてもあまり不自由なく生活できる東京は、その象徴ともいえるだろう。都内における若年層の運転免許保有率減少は顕著で、1991年にはほぼ7割5分だったものが、現在では6割強。その上、若年層の人口そのものが減っている。厳しい逆風の中で、世間のトレンドとは明らかに反比例し、直近の業績が高度成長期まで含めても最高の状態になっている。それが、「東京車人」のマークで知られている武蔵境自動車教習所だ。

　アロハシャツを着た教官が、笑顔でドアを開けてくれる。自分に合った教官をタブレットで簡単に予約できる。空き時間は、漫画が読めたり、英会話が学べたりする。マッサージで身体をいやし、ネイルの手入れまでできる。子どもを託児所に預けておくと、帰り際には子どもが母親の服を引っ張り、泣いて嫌がる——。アンケートを取れば、実に98％の卒業生が肯定的な評価を返してくれる。そして、新たにやってくる入所者の半数は、既卒者からの紹介だ。それだけではない。ミニコンサートにフリーマーケット。年末には餅つき、そして夏には花火が上がる。老いも若きも、教習に関係のない人まで笑顔で教習所にやってくる。すでに、この地域の風物詩にさえなっている。

　ここは、温泉施設でも、テーマパークでもない。なのに、社員からはおもてなしのアイデアが湧き出す。なぜこんな発想が出てくるのか。だが、髙橋勇会長の圧倒的な「おもてなし経営」は、波乱と苦難からのスタートだった。

| The Ascent of The Japan Brand 03 | Musashisakai Driving School Co., LTD. | Isamu Takahashi |

A Driving School With a 98percent Satisfaction Rate, and Many Referrals

When I heard of a driving school in Tokyo that continues to grow even now, with better financial results than ever, I found it hard to believe. My intuition told me that this was most unlikely.

The falling birth rate is significant, as is the number of young people not interested in driving. This is epitomized by Tokyo, where not having a car does not restrict you in anyway. Particularly striking is the decrease in the rate of young people becoming licensed drivers in Tokyo: in 1991 it was 75percent, which has now dropped to just over 60percent. On top of this, the actual population of young people is shrinking. Amid these adverse winds, Musashisakai Driving School, known by the "Tokyo Shajin" mark, is enjoying its best results ever – ever better than during the era of of rapid economic growth – which is in contrast to current trends.

The driving instructor, rocking a Hawaiian shirt, opens the door with a smile. You can use a tablet computer to easily reserve the instructor that best suits you. In between lessons, you can read manga comics, learn English conversation, heal your body with a massage, or get your nails done. Parents leave their kids in the creche area, and when it is time to go home the kids cry and beg to stay a little longer. Customer surveys shows that 98percent of graduates give a positive feedback; half of new learners are introduced by alumni. This is not all. There's a mini concert and flea market. *Mochi Tsuki* (rice-cake pounding)　at New Year, fireworks in the summer. Young and old happily flock to the driving school, many of whom have no connection to it. Already, its events have become a regional fixture in the summer.

This is not a hot spring facility, neither is it a theme park. Yet ideas for hospitality spring forth from employees. Where does this inspiration come from? However, this "hospitable management" approach of chairman Isamu Takahashi was born from hardship and troubles.

叔父の「仇」を討つ方法

　新宿駅から中央線で20分弱。武蔵境は武蔵野市の西側にある住宅を中心とした街だ。1960年、まさに高度経済成長期の入り口に当たる年、この地に武蔵境自動車教習所がオープンした。4年後の東京オリンピックに向けてインフラ整備が進み、経済成長によって庶民でもクルマに手が届くようになる、モータリゼーションの花開くまっただ中に、今ある資源を有効活用し、日本社会への貢献と成長の一翼を担いたいという想いが芽生えたのが、創業のきっかけだった。

　経営は順風満帆だった。創業者は社員からの人気も高く、自信に満ちた経営者だった。だが1988年に労働組合が結成され雰囲気は一変。突如赤旗が林立する異様な職場と化す。連日の厳しい団体交渉に疲れ切った創業者は勇退することになり、翌1989年4月1日、髙橋の叔父が二代目を引き継いだ。だが、翌4月2日、たった1日社長を務めた後に、叔父は自ら命を絶ってしまった。「私が経営者として最初にした仕事は、叔父の亡骸を警察署から引き取り、お葬式を出すことだったのです」

　いずれは教習所の経営を引き継ぐつもりではいたものの、当時大手生命保険会社のサラリーマンだった髙橋にとって、それはあまりにも突然で、ショッキングな出来事だった。葬儀の間、髙橋の頭には、すぐに教習所を畳むこと以外、何も浮かばなかった。嘆き悲しむ親族の姿。とてもではないがもう続けられない。一刻も早く負の連鎖を断ち切りたい。バブル景気のピーク期、十分な利益が出ている企業を清算したいという経営者などどこにもいなかったから、弁護士も会計士もお互いに顔を見合わせていた。それでも決意は揺るがず、1ヵ月も経たないうちに、いつでも清算できる準備が整えられた。これでようやく、叔父の

Avenging the Death of his Uncle

Just under 20 minutes from Shinjuku Station on the Chuo Line. Musashi Sakai is a mainly residential area in the western part of Musashino City. In 1960, the year that marked the onset of the era of high economic growth, Musashisakai Driving School opened there. The rolling out of infrastructure was continuing apace for the Tokyo Olympics that were to be held four years later. And due to the rapid economic growth, cars had become affordable to the masses. During this phase, which was right in the middle of an era when motorization was booming, Musashisakai Driving School was established. It was born from the concept of making efficient use of resources at hand to contribute to Japanese society and to play a part in its growth.

Management was sailing smoothly. The founder was highly popular with employees and a very confident manager. However, the environment suddenly changed in 1988 with the formation of labor union; the workplace was suddenly bristling with red flags. Exhausted by daily collective negotiations, the founder took honorable retirement, meaning that a year later on April 1, 1989, Takahashi's uncle became the second-generation president. However, on April 2, just one day after becoming president, Takahashi's uncle took his own life.
"The first job that I did as manager was to collect my uncle's corpse from the police station and to take it to the funeral."

This was all rather a sudden and shocking series of events for Takahashi, who while on one hand was intending to take on the management of the driving school some day, was at the time employed in a desk job at a major life insurance company. During the funeral, Takahashi could not think of any other option but to close the driving school. Around him were relatives, wallowing in grief. He simply could not continue. He wanted to sever the negative chain of events as soon as possible. During the peak years of the bubble economy, there wasn't a single manager who wanted to liquidate a company that was sufficiently profitable, and so the lawyers and accountants exchanged

「仇」を討てる。朝方の誰もいない社長室で、初めて髙橋の心の中に、わずかな心の余裕が生まれた。

奢りと慢心を断ち切る

　後は、自分のタイミングで会社を清算できる。地価の高騰もあって、通常の3倍という手厚い退職金を全社員に支払ってもなお、今後一族が食べていくのに必要な資産は残せるはずだ。これでようやく、静かな日々がやってくる。そう思うと、あの日以来両肩にのしかかっていた重荷がすっと下りていくような、初めての感覚を味わうことができた。髙橋の中に、怒涛の数週間と、そこに至る経緯を振り返る余裕が生まれた。

「そもそも、どうしてこんなことになってしまったのか。初めてそこに考えが及んだのです」

　労働組合を結成すること自体は法で保障された権利であり、経営側からとやかく言う筋合いのものではない。ただ、仕事そっちのけで連日団体交渉を要求し、言いたい放題の主張を繰り返す有り様は異様で、眼を覆うばかりだった。しかし、彼らが大声を上げている現状には背景があった。より直截に表現すれば、「プロ」が外部から入り込み、組合を巧みにオーガナイズしていた。

　叔父の仇を討つために、会社ごとなくして労働組合を断ち切る。確かに、それで平穏な日々は確実にやってくるだろう。でも、本当は他にもやり方があるのではないか。外から組合に入り込まれる隙を与えてしまったのは、経営側に奢りや慢心、独断的に過ぎる意識があったのではないか。社員全員の本音を聞き、しっかり自分たちにフィードバックしていたのだろうか。叔父の仇を討つ行為とは、もしかしたら会社をなくすことではなく、会社を継続し、良いものにして

quizzical looks. This did not shake Takahashi's resolve, and in less than a month, preparations were in place to liquidate the company at any time. Finally, he could avenge the "ruination" of his uncle. Alone in the president's office one morning, Takahashi felt a sense of relief creeping in for the first time.

Cutting free from Pride and Self-Conceit

  He would liquidate the company in his own time. The local land price was high, and even if he paid all employees three times the normal retirement benefits, there would still be enough assets left to keep his family well fed and clothed. At last, peaceful days would return. Upon thinking this, the heavy weight that had been bearing down on his shoulders since that day suddenly was lifted for the first time. Takahashi now had the mental breathing space to reflect on the chaotic few weeks and the process leading up to it.
"How did we ever end up in this predicament in the first place? It was the first time I was able to reflect on it all."

  The act of forming a labor union is a right protected by law, and the management has no business complaining about it. However, it had turned into a bizarre shambles, with management having to completely ignore work due to the daily demands for negotiations andrepeatedly fielding complaints.

  Meanwhile, there was a background to their making such a big fuss. To put it simply, a "pro" had come in from the outside, who was able to skillfully control the union.

  If he wanted to avenge his uncle's ruination, he could get rid of the company and in doing so destroy the labor union. That would mean the return of a peaceful life, but perhaps there was another approach. Could the gap through which this outsider had entered the union existed because of pride and conceit on the management side, and because of their overly dogmatic mindset? Had the managers provided open communication channels to employees and taken into account their feedback? To avenge his uncle's ruination, rather than getting rid of the company, perhaps he could continue it and take it in a

いくことなのではないか……。
「よし。いつでもやめられるなら、もう一度やってみよう」
　これが現在に至る「おもてなし経営」のスタートだった。

教習所は何を売っているのか?

　ただ、この時点で切り替わったのは、髙橋の頭の中だけだった。それを社員が受け入れてくれるかは、あくまで別問題である。
「今のような意識を作り上げるまでに、10年かかりました」
　髙橋はそう振り返る。免許取得のために仕方なく通う教習所から、イベント目当てに遊びに行く教習所、地域のワンダーランドとなるまでには、どのような意識改革があったのだろう。自動車教習所の存在する意義、そしてそこで働く意義とは、いったい何なのか。今に至るまで、大半の教習所は、そのような想いを巡らせたことはないに違いない。顧客も、仕事や生活で免許が必要だから、多少問題があろうと家から近い教習所に通い、やり過ごしてくれる。通常は人生で二度教習所に通うことはないから、不満を漏らしても仕方がない。
「当時の武蔵境自動車教習所も、創業の想いを忘れてしまっていた。だから経営者は金儲けだけを、社員は楽をして給料をもらうことだけを考えていました」
　教習所は、いったい何を売っているのか？　髙橋はまず、こう宣言した。
「教習所は廃業し、私たちはサービス業になる。そういう視点で、私はこの会社を経営していきます」
　これからは、免許を取得するという経験を売る。しかし、社員たちの反応は、苦々しいか、何も響かないかのふたつに大別された。組合の突き上げは相変わらずだった。髙橋の姿を見つけては取り囲み、あれこれ叫び、容赦なく批判

positive direction....

"Right. If I can quit at any moment, I might just give it one more go."

This was the start of the "hospitable management" that continues to this day.

What Exactly does a Driving School Sell?

At this juncture, a shift had taken place only inside Takahashi's head. Whether employees would endorse this or not was a separate issue.

"To get to the frame of mind we have today, took 10 years."

Takahashi looks back. What sort of change in thinking took place in order to go from a driving school where people go because they have to get their license, to a driving school that people come to with events in mind, a veritable local wonderland? What is the actual purpose of a driving school, and what is the significance of working in one? Up until now, it is safe to say that the bulk of driving schools will never have considered this notion. Customers need to get their license for work and daily life, and commute to the nearest school even if it is not perfect, and get on with it. Normally, people do not go to a driving school twice in their lives, so there is no point in grumbling about it.

"The Musashisakai Driving School at that time had forgotten its roots. So, managers only thought about making money, and employees just wanted to coast along getting a salary."

What on earth does a driving school sell? First and foremost, Takahashi made this declaration:

"We will abandon the concept of a driving school, and become a service provider. I will manage this company from this perspective."

From now on, they would sell the experience of gaining a driving license. However, the reactions of employees could be broadly divided into those who were bitter, and those who were nonplussed.

The up-thrust from the union was as unrelenting as ever. They would find Takahashi and encircle him, showering him in scathing comments and criticism.

の言葉を浴びせる。そうではない社員たちも、何も新しい行動を起こす様子はなかった。

　苦悩していたある日、髙橋の頭にひらめきが生まれた。
「私は、この泥沼の環境の中で、過去の経営を反省し、社員を幸せにしたいという想いを確固たるものにしました。そして、やり方や方向性は異なるが、彼らも自分たち自身が幸せになりたいという想いは共通であることに、気がついたのです」

　企業である以上、労使という関係性から脱することはできないが、教習所には、経営者と従業員以外にも、通ってくださるお客様がいて、隣人や地域社会の存在だってあるはずだ。経営者対従業員という関係だけで考えていくと、大事なことを忘れてしまう。一人ひとりの社員が幸せになるためには、もっと広い視野から考える、内向きな視点からの転換が必要なのだ。

　お客様にはそれぞれの人生がある。自動車免許の取得は、大切なライフイベントのひとつだ。そして、この教習所の周りに住まいがあって、地域社会を構成している。多くの人が、より良い街を作ろうと自分たちにできる努力を人知れず続けている。時には武蔵境自動車教習所が地域の施設を使用させてもらうこともある。自分たちの存在は、地域社会あってのものなのだ。お互いに視線を外に向ける。自分たちの置かれている環境が理解できれば、経営者対従業員というだけでなく、顧客・地域社会対オール武蔵境自動車教習所という認識も生まれるはずだ。ここから現在の武蔵境自動車教習所を支える、「共尊共栄」という経営理念、そして「社員満足」「顧客満足」「地域社会貢献」という3つの柱が形作られ、これらを土台にした改革がスタートしていったのだ。

Employees who did not fall into this camp, meanwhile, did not do anything new.

Distressed, one day Takahashi had a brain wave.

"Stuck in this quagmire, I looked back on past management and firmed my resolve that I wanted to make the employees happy. I began to notice that, while their methods and direction were different, they also shared the desire to become happy too."

As a company, you cannot remove the relationship of labor and management; however, within a driving school, apart from managers and employees, there are the customers who come to learn and there are also people living nearby and the local community. If you think only in terms of managers vs. employees, you forget something very important. In order for each employee to become content, you need to have a wider field of vision, and shift away from an inward-looking perspective.

Customers each have their respective lives. Acquiring a driving license is a significant life event. Furthermore, there are people living around the driving school, forming the local community. Most people continue to strive to make it a better place, unnoticed by others. There are times when Musashisakai Driving School makes use of facilities in the community. The school owes its existence to the local community. Both sides divert their glances outward. If each side can understand the situation that they have been put in, rather than managers vs employees, it should be possible to create the perception of customers/local community vs a united Musashisakai Driving School. This marked the start of the management principle of "mutual respect, mutual prosperity" which underpins the Musashisakai Driving School of today, as well as the forming of the three pillars of "employee satisfaction," "customer satisfaction," and "contribution to the local society," upon which the reinvention could take place.

The Root of the Service Industry is a Feeling of Happiness

How should he go about connecting with the local community, and

サービス業の根幹は幸福感

　地域社会とどうつながり、貢献していくのか。髙橋の想いを初めて形にしたイベントが、1989年12月28日に開かれた「謝恩餅つき大会」だった。

　失意と怒りの日々からわずか8ヵ月。髙橋の表情は明るかった。

「50キロのお餅を用意したら、300人くらいお客様が来てくださった。うれしかったね。大成功でした」

　組合員の中からも、何人か手伝ってくれる人が現れた。そしてこの日、髙橋の想いは確信に変わった。

「社員もお客様も、そして私も喜んでいた。そこに理屈はありません。楽しいこと、いいことをしているから笑顔が自然に出てくる。お客様が喜ぶ姿を見れば、自分も幸福感を得てもっともっと喜ばせたいと考えるようになる。教習所はサービス業になれるのです」

　確信を得て改革のスピードが加速していく。翌年、今度は花火大会を企画した。これが地域と武蔵境自動車教習所をつなぐ決定的な出来事となった。

「お騒がせするわけですから、周辺のお宅を一軒一軒回りながらご挨拶し、無

地域社会に貢献するという想いを実現するために開かれた「謝恩餅つき大会」は、今では毎年末の恒例行事となり、多くの人々で賑わう
Mochi Tsuki (the rice-cake pounding party) was initially held to realize the desire to contribute to the local community; it is now a regular event held at the end of every year.

contributing to it? The first event that gave form to Takahashi's idea was the "Giving Thanks *Mochi Tsuki* (rice-cake pounding) Party" held on December 28, 1989.

Only eight months had passed since the days of adversity and anger. Takahashi's features had lightened.

"I prepared 50kg of *mochi* (rice cake), and about 300 customers came. That was great. It was a big success."

Several people from within also came the labor union to help out. And on that day, Takahashi's feeling changed into a strong conviction.

"Employees were happy, customers were happy, and I was happy. There is no theory behind it. If you are doing something fun, something good, you naturally end up with a smile on your face. When you see customers enjoying themselves, you feel happy yourself and want to make them even happier. The driving school can become a hospitality industry."

Having reached this conviction, the pace of reform accelerated. The following year, he organized a fireworks party. This was a decisive event in connecting the local community with Musashisakai Driving School.

"We were going to make a lot of noise, so we went around each house in the neighborhood to let them know that they could come for free. It was a good opportunity to get to know everybody in person."

They put up tents and prepared stalls including a shooting gallery, yo-yo and fried noodles. Naturally, all the service was provided by staff. On top of this, gorgeous fireworks lit up the sky and made lasting summer memories. There were shouts of glee.

"Although exhausted, employees were mentally recharged and their eyes were sparkling. They were thanked over and over again by customers, and I could see their mindset gradually changing."

The fireworks party gets bigger every year, and is these days called the "Summer Festival." Together with the Giving Thanks *Mochi Tsuki* (rice-cake pounding) Party," it has become an event that colors the season in Musashi Sakai.

料で遊んでいただける旨を説明しました。皆さんのお顔を見る機会を得られたのです」

　テントを張り、射的やヨーヨー、焼きそばなどの出店も用意した。もちろんサービスは社員が行う。そこに、夏の思い出を切り取る大きな花火が輝く。歓声が上がる。

「社員は、身体は疲れていても、気持ちは充実して、眼はキラキラしていた。何度も『ありがとう』という言葉をかけられて、どんどん意識が変わっていく様子がわかりました」

　花火大会は年々規模が大きくなり、今は「サマーフェスティバル」と名前を変えた。謝恩餅つき大会とともに、武蔵境の季節を彩るイベントになった。

社員との強い信頼を作る方法

「団体交渉はもう結構です。社長に一切お任せします」

　社長就任から10年目の春闘。髙橋は組合側の代表からこんな言葉をもらった。ようやく最初のチャレンジが終わったのだ。そして「社員満足」「顧客満足」「地域社会貢献」の3つの柱における改革もさらなる広がりを見せていく。

　社員満足を高めるために、社員教育を徹底し、仕事に対する意味や価値観の向上、やりがいのある職場環境作りを行った。顧客満足を高めるためには、常にお客様目線で「お客様に何ができるか」を現場が考え、接客マナーの向上を図ることで、お客様に寄り添った対応ができるようになった。教習の待ち時間も楽しんでいただくため、ネイルやマッサージなどの多彩なサービスやイベントを実施した。また、卒業後の練習車両の貸し出しなど無期限のアフターフォローも充実させた。地域社会貢献については、「地域への感謝と貢献が会社

How to Win the Firm Trust of Employees

"We don't need any more collective bargaining. We will leave it all to you."

In his 10th year of the annual spring wage negotiations since becoming president, Takahashi received these words from the union representative. At last, the first challenge was over. Also, reform was starting to pick up based on the three pillars of "employee satisfaction," "customer satisfaction" and "contributing to local society"

To raise employee satisfaction, he implemented thorough employee education, enhanced the significance and sense of value of doing the job, and created a workplace environment with purpose. To raise customer satisfaction, he got people on the frontline to be more customer-oriented and to think "what can I do for the customer." And also improved customer service in order to enable employees to engage with the customers in a way that is more considerate of their feelings. To let customers enjoy their waiting time, he implemented a diverse range of services including a massage and a nail salon, as well as events. He also insisted on unlimited after-care by lending practice vehicles to graduates. To further contribute to the local community, based on the notion that "gratitude and contribution to the community will power up the company's development," he begun morning cleaning activities, opened up the driving practice course for events such as the aforementioned fireworks and rice-cake pounding parties, held charity events that could be enjoyed by all ages, and in doing so created a driving school that was open to the community.

These various initiatives bore fruit, with the corporate results of Musashisakai Driving School maintaining an even keel. The level of salaries and bonuses were high compared to those of competitors, meaning that a sense of satisfaction pervaded the company. Moreover, based on his experiences and beliefs, Takahashi made all financial statements freely available to the union, something that there is usually no need to publicly disclose. On top of this, he

の発展の源」という考えのもと、朝の清掃活動をはじめ、教習コースを開放した前述の花火大会や餅つき大会など、子どもからお年寄りまで楽しんでいただけるチャリティイベントを開催し、地域に開かれた教習所作りを行った。

　さまざまな取り組みが功を奏し、武蔵境自動車教習所の業績は、順調に推移していた。同業他社と比較しても給与・賞与の水準は高くなり、納得感が広がった。加えて髙橋は、これまでの経験と信念から、通常は公開する必要のない財務諸表まで、完全に組合側にオープンにすることにした。さらに、会社として労働分配率を50％にすると公言したのだ。労働分配率とは、簡単にいえば企業活動の結果手元に残った利益の何割を人件費として従業員に還元するかという指標である。通常社員に対して前もって約束することはないし、ましてその計算のもととなる財務諸表まで誰でも見られる企業は、相当に特殊といえる。

「私の年収がいくらなのかだって、簡単にわかりますよ」

　髙橋の言葉は決して大げさではない。こうして、信頼関係は深まっていった。

　1995年、武蔵境自動車教習所は創立35周年を迎えていた。その年の忘年会で、髙橋はこう宣言する。

「5年後、創立40周年には、東京で一番の教習所になろうよ！」

　まだ、呆気に取られている社員のほうが多数派だった。しかし、眼を輝かせる社員も少なくなかった。そのためには、7000人の入所者を迎え入れる必要がある。ではどうすればいいのか？ 5年後、残念ながら武蔵境自動車教習所は、東京で2番目の成績に終わった。ただし、成長した分の分配は、しっかり社員に与えられた。そして、もうひとつの「報酬」が、企業と社員をさらに豊かにしていく。

publicly declared that the company's labor share would be 50percent. Labor share, put simply, is an index of the ratio of profits derived from corporate activities that are returned to employees. Normally there are no promises made with employees in advance, and beyond that it is extremely rare for a company to let anybody in the company view the financial statements upon which this ratio is calculated.

"You can easily find out how much my annual salary is."

Takahashi was certainly not exaggerating. With this, employee trust in him only deepened.

In 1995, Musashisakai Driving School celebrated its 35th year since establishment. At the end of year party, Takahashi made the following declaration:

"In five years, in our 40th year, together we can become the top driving school in Tokyo!"

The majority of employees were taken aback by this. However, there were many employees whose eyes lit up. In order to do this, they would have to take in 7000 learners. How could they go about doing it? Five years later, Musashisakai Driving School unfortunately had only the second-best results performance in Tokyo. That said, proceeds from growth were fairly distributed among employees. Furthermore, another kind of "compensation" enriched the company and employees even more.

小さな子どものいる主婦に重宝されている無料託児所
The free nursery is highly convenient for housewives with young children.

湧き出るアイデア

　儲けている時は独り占めして、傾いてくれば即リストラ。そんな会社ではないことが理解されてくると、社員たちは思わぬ能力を発揮し始めるようになった。より成長するには、どうすればいいのか。自分にできることは何か。それを、社員自らが考えるカルチャーが出来上がったのだ。

「3000万円の予算を使って地域社会にどう喜んでいただくかを考えるのも、通常の教習料金の倍額をいただくとしたらどのようなサービスを提供すればいいかを考えるのも、今では全部社員です」

　時代は変わっていく。昨日のことは過去のこと。より良くするためにはどんどん考え、変えていこう。そう髙橋が言うだけで、ネイルサロンやマッサージコーナーができていく。託児所が充実して、今まで免許を持っていなかった主婦層の口コミで、どんどん高年齢層の入所者が増えてくる。花火大会などのイベントで得た収益は、すべて地域や福祉団体へのチャリティに還元する。つまり、経営的には100％持ち出しだ。それでも、自分が社会に貢献しているという得がたい体験を味わえる。

　社員の自主的な姿勢は、具体的な取り組みとして花開いていく。武蔵境自動車教習所では、幅広いお客様の多様なニーズに応えるべく、1989年から戦略的に女性社員の採用や高齢者の再雇用を積極的に実施。特に、女性社員の採用は業界の先駆けとなり、現在では全体の45％を女性が占めている。経営理念の一番の柱である「社員満足」の向上を図るため、生涯職場作りと、年齢、性別等に関係なく「出る釘は伸ばす」という人事理念のもと、やる気がある社員には資格取得のための教育などチャンスを与えている。また、女性社員を商品開発やプロジェクトリーダーに積極的に抜擢することで、幹部

An Upwelling of Ideas

Monopolize when making money, swiftly restructure when things start to decline. When employees realize that it is not that kind of company, they unexpectedly become able to demonstrate their abilities What needs to be done to grow further? What can we do ourselves? A culture was in place under which employees could think about this for themselves.
"These days, when it comes to thinking about how to use a 30 million yen budget to delight the local community, or about what sort of service we need to provide in order to receive twice the normal amount of instruction fee, it is the employees who do all the thinking."

Eras change. What happened yesterday is in the past. To make things better, think, and enact change. By Takahashi simply uttering these words, a nail salon and massage corner appeared. The day the nursery was completed to perfection, and through word-of-mouth by housewives who up until now did not have a driving license, the number of elderly learners increased thick and fast. Profits made from events such as the fireworks display are all returned to the community and welfare organizations in the form of charity. In other words, from a management perspective, a 100percent carryout. Nevertheless, this makes it possible to experience what it feels like to contribute to the community.

The autonomous mindset of employees blossoms in the form of concrete initiatives. So as to respond to the diverse needs of a wide pool of customers, Musashisakai Driving School has, since 1989, strategically hired female employees and proactively implemented re-employment for senior citizens. In particular, they are a pioneer when it comes to hiring of female employees, who make up 45percent of the current workforce. In order to fulfill the top-priority management pillar of improving "employee satisfaction", as well as creating lifetime workplace, ambitious employees are given education and other opportunities for acquiring qualifications, based on the human resources principle of "nails that stick out will grow," irrespective of age or gender. Also,

候補としての育成を実施している。

「IT-VIP」というハイグレードサービスは、女性社員の活躍によりその販売が3年前と比較し131％増加したという。通常のベーシックプランに比べ、さまざまな特典がついているが、比較すると10万円以上割高なプランである。このプランの価値を顧客によりわかりやすく伝えるため、女性社員が主体となって、消費者の視点でのパンフレットデザインの見直し、顧客のニーズを聞き出すためのロールプレイ研修や説明方法の改善、既存の顧客への手書きメッセージの配布など、満足度向上のための多くの工夫や改善を実施した。その結果、顧客のニーズに合った提案が受け入れられ、実際に利用した顧客の満足度も大幅に向上した。ネイルやマッサージサービスなど女性社員発案のサービス提供により、女性のお客様も増加。ひいてはすべてのお客様にとって気持ち良い環境となり、日常的に改善提案が生まれる職場になっている。

社員が満足していれば、ビジネスも地域貢献もうまくいく

今、武蔵境自動車教習所の経営理念を支える3つの柱は、前述したように、シンプルな3つの言葉で表現されている。

「社員満足」「顧客満足」「地域社会貢献」

社員が満足していれば、顧客を満たし、地域に貢献できる。この原則を毎朝確認し、全員と握手して一体感を高める。こうした一体感は、顧客にも伝わっている。そもそも教習所に通う主な層は、おおむね大学生の年齢に相当する。武蔵境自動車教習所で免許を取得した学生の中には、就職先としてこの企業を選んでくれる人も少なくないというのだ。

the company proactively selects and promotes female employees to product development positions or as project leaders in order to nurture them into candidates for executive positions.

For the high-grade "IT-VIP" service, the active role played by female employees resulted in sales of this service increasing 131percent in three years. Compared to the basic plan, there are various fringe benefits with this plan, which costs over 100,000 yen and is somewhat pricey in comparison. In order to better communicate the value of this plan to customers, female employees took the initiative in revising the design of pamphlets from a consumer point of view, engaged in role-play training to improve their way of inquiring about customer needs. They also improved their way of explaining things, distributed hand-written messages to existing customers, and pursued various other initiatives and improvements to increase customer satisfaction. As a result, proposals fitting customer needs were accepted, significantly elevating the level of satisfaction of the customers who accepted the proposals. By providing nail and massage services devised by female employees, the number of female customers increased. Indeed, a more comfortable environment for all customers prevailed, as well as a workplace where suggestions for improvement are forthcoming on a daily basis.

If Employees are Happy, Business and Community Contribution will Thrive

As previously explained, the three pillars underpinning the management principles of Musashisakai Driving School can be expressed in three simple phrases:
"Employee Satisfaction" "Customer Satisfaction" "Contribution to Local Society."

If employees are satisfied, they will in turn satisfy customers, and contribute to the community. Every morning Takahashi re-confirms these principles, and engenders a sense of unity by shaking everybody by the hand.

「ありがたいことです。新卒者の採用は積極的に行っているのですが、かつての自動車教習所という業種では考えられなかったレベルの優秀な学生さんに関心を持っていただけているし、実際に入社してくれています」

まるで、ディズニーランドやスターバックスのような話ではないか。顧客として味わった感動、経営理念への共感と共鳴を抱いた人が、仲間になってくれるのだから。髙橋は、彼らを部下として見られなくなってきている自分を自覚しているという。

「特に若い人を見ると、『社会からのお預かりもの』と感じるようになりました」

きっちりとした社会人にする。それが武蔵境自動車教習所の責任で、その結果、転職されても一向にかまわない。他のことにチャレンジしたくなったら、その発想自体を褒めてあげたい。もちろん、さまざまな経験を積んで戻ってくることも大歓迎だという。花火に代表されるイベントも、地域住民の心をつかんでいる。この地域の住民にとって、8月の最後の土曜といえば教習所の花火の日なのだ。子どもは宿題とにらめっこしながら、あるいは放り出して教習所に駆け込む。さらに、離れて暮らしている子や孫が、花火目当てに遠くから武蔵境にやってくる例もあるそうだ。彼らが、免許を取ろうと思ったら？　武蔵境以

8月後半に開催される花火大会当日の武蔵境駅周辺は、花火目当ての人々で賑やかになるという
On the day in late August when the fireworks display is held, the area around Musashi Sakai Station is bustling with people who come especially for the event.

This sense of unity is conveyed to customers. In the first place, the main demographic of people who come to driving school are those around the age of university students. Among students who acquired their license at Musashisakai Driving School, there are more than a few who choose it as their employer when they enter the workforce.

"This is most pleasing. We proactively recruit new graduates, and attract and employ elite students who we would never have once associated with the business category of driving school."

This sounds more like a tale you would hear about Disneyland or Starbucks. People who had a very positive experience as customers and who endorse the company's management principles and ways, want to come onboard. Takahashi admits that he is conscious of himself no longer being able to see them as underlings:

"With regard to youngsters in particular, I have come to see them in terms of 'an entrustment from society.'"

They make them into steady-handed members of society. This is the responsibility of Musashisakai Driving School, and it matters not one iota if they wish to change jobs. If they want to go and pursue a new challenge, then Takahashi encourages this very attitude. Of course, they are very welcome to go and acquire all sorts of experiences before coming back again. Events typified by the fireworks display also play a part in winning over the local residents. For residents in this community, the last Saturday of August means only one thing, the driving school fireworks display. Some children are engrossed with their homework at the party while others throw it aside. Apparently, there are even cases where children and grandchildren who live far away make the journey all the way to Musashi Sakai just to join in the party. What if they want to get their license one day? Will they ever venture outside of Musashi Sakai, I wonder.

Spreading "Feeling" from Musashi Sakai

Presently, Musashisakai Driving School is adopting an expansion policy

外に行くことがあるのだろうか。

武蔵境から「想い」を広げていく

　武蔵境自動車教習所は今、成長のため、そして自ら見出した教習所の存在価値を広げていくため、拡大政策を始めようとしている。きっかけは、2012年に香川県坂出市の教習所を買収したことだった。

　当初は再建に取り組む経営者の相談に乗っているだけのつもりだった。だが次第に業績が悪化し、買収してほしいと依頼された。あまり気は進まなかったものの、そこで働いている人の姿が、かつての武蔵境の情景と重なった。地域雇用を守るためになるならと引き受けることにした。昔ながらの居丈高な教官たち。お客様の快適さはほとんど考えられていないばかりか、売上高アップのための教習時間オーバーが横行している。旧態依然とした場所だった。怒りを通り越して、悲しく、恥ずかしくなった。それから3年。武蔵境で培ったノウハウを注入し、環境を一変させ、各種のイベントを開催している。合宿免許の呼び込みも力を入れ、徐々に業績は改善を見せている。

　今まで、同業他社がどうなっているかなど、あまり考えてはこなかった。しかし、この業界の社会におけるあまりの貢献度の低さに愕然として、意識が変わったという。シナジー効果が生まれやすい関東近郊を中心に、今後数校を買収し、武蔵境流のおもてなしで業界のイメージを変えていきたいと考えている。警察でも、免許センターでもない。お客様の人生を見ながら仕事をする。そして、必要か必要でないかは、社会が決める。そのレベルでのチャレンジが、これからの武蔵境自動車教習所の進む道だ。

in order to grow, and also in order to spread out the existential value of the driving school that they have hit upon. The catalyst for this was the purchase of a driving school in Sakaide City in Kagawa Prefecture in 2012.

To begin with, Takahashi was consulting with the manager who was in the process of re-generating the driving school. However, results went from bad to worse, and he asked Takahashi to buy the school. Although he was not particularly interested, the sight of the people working there gave him a flashback to how Musashi Sakai used to look. He accepted the offer to purchase the school, in the belief that it might safeguard local employment. High-handed instructors from the old days, with almost no regard for the comfort of customers, deliberately exceeding the allotted lesson time in order to beef up sales were widespread. It was a place that was stuck in the past. Rather than anger, Takahashi felt sad, and then ashamed. Three years have passed since then. Injecting the know-how built up in Musashi Sakai, he radically changed the environment, organizing various events. He focused energies on calling customers for residential courses, gradually steering performance back into a good direction.

Until now, Takahashi had not given much thought to what competitors were up to. However, shocked at the paltry level of contribution to society made by this industry, he changed his mind. Centered on the Kanto Region where it is easy to build synergies, Takahashi intends to purchase several driving schools, and to use the Musashi Sakai style of hospitality to change the image of the industry. This is not a police station, nor a license center. Perform a job while observing the lives of customers. Whether this is necessary or not, society will be the judge. The road ahead for Musashisakai Driving School is one of such lofty challenge.

The Day that "Tokyo Shajin" became Disneyland

There are Musashisakai Driving School advertising boards along the Chuo Line, centered on Musashi Sakai Station. Affixed to these is a 3-D slanting

「東京車人」がディズニーランドになった日

　武蔵境駅のある中央線を中心に、武蔵境自動車教習所の看板が設置されている。そこには立体的で斜めになっているハンコが捺されていて、「東京車人」と書かれている。印象に残っている人も少なくないはずだ。自動車教習所の広告において、こうした看板は昔も今も高い訴求力を持っているそうだ。実はこのキャッチコピーを考えたのも、社員なのだという。
「広告代理店にお願いして考えてもらったら、『関東車人』という案が出てきた。すると、まずは東京で一番を目指すのだから、東京のほうがエネルギーが高くていいよね、という意見が出て、他の社員にもおおむね好評だったんです」
　そう言って、髙橋は眼を細める。東京都内で自動車学校を卒業した人数は、2014年で12万人弱。ピーク時は28万人だったというのだから、6割減という驚くべきシュリンクである。その中で、武蔵境自動車教習所が創業以来最高レベルの業績を残しているのだから、すでに武蔵境、東京車人のブランド力は、顧客の動向によって、社会の評価によって決定づけられているといえるだろう。
「私たちはコストを抑えない。それ以上に売上を上げていけばいい、という発想でやっています」
　髙橋の言葉は、やはりディズニーランドを思い起こさせる。ブランドができてしまえば、顧客は期待通りでは感動はしない。ショーでゲストをどうびっくりさせるか、もっと感動させるかを考える際は、アイデア優先でコストはいったん度外視し、最後の最後、どう考えても無理なものだけを除外する。こうした発想でなければ、たったひとつのアトラクションに200億円なんてかけられない。
　確かに、自動車教習所という産業のパイが今後も減っていくことは否めない。しかし、退屈な教習所をディズニーランドに変えた「武蔵境」という考え方自

stamp-seal, displaying the words "Tokyo Shajin." Many people will recall seeing this. When it comes to adverts for driving schools, apparently these sorts of advertising boards have a lot of appeal power, both now and in the past. In fact, the employees were the ones who came up with this logo.

"When we asked an advertising agency, they suggested "Kanto Shajin" (Kanto is the large plain in the Eastern part of Japan where Tokyo is located). At that point, someone offered their opinion that as we are aiming to be number one in Tokyo, the word Tokyo is more appropriate and more effervescent; most other employees were in agreement."

Saying this, Takahashi narrows his eyes. The number of people graduating from driving schools in the Tokyo Metropolitan Area was just under 120,000 in 2014. At the peak, this number was 280,000 people, meaning an astonishing decrease to the tune of 60percent. Amid these conditions, Musashisakai Driving School has posted record high financial results since its establishment – suggesting that the brand power of Musashi Sakai and Tokyo Shajin has already been determined by customer trends and the assessment by society.

"We do not cut costs. We operate on the notion that we should achieve sales above and beyond our costs."

Takahashi's words seem reminiscent of Disneyland. Once you have a brand in place, customers cannot feel excited if things happen in line with their expectations. When considering how to surprise guests through a show, or how to make them feel more excited, you prioritize ideas and temporarily disregard cost. At the very end, you only get rid of that which is absolutely unfeasible. If you don't think in this way, you cannot expend 20 billion yen on one attraction.

Without doubt, the size of the driving school industry pie will only shrink from now on. However, if it is possible to imbue a brand with the very "Musashi Sakai" approach, which transformed a dull driving school into a Disneyland, the opportunities are limitless.

体をブランドにできれば、チャンスは無限に広がっていく。

できることは、まだまだたくさんある

　髙橋の今後の関心ごとは、自動運転だという。どういうことなのだろうか。
「私は、自動運転の開発と普及は国策として進んでいくと思います。あと5年、10年でかなり形が見えてくるはずです。日本だけでなく、欧米でも事情は同じ。グーグルのドライバーレスカーの開発も進んでいますよね。教習所業界には困ったことかもしれませんが、これは、より安全な自動車社会を望む世の中の要請ですから」
　その時、自動車教習所のカリキュラムは、半分、3分の1になるかもしれない。どう生き残るのか。
「実は、あまり怖さは感じていません。今は教習所が本業ですから、自分たちのやり方で雇用を増やし、社会に貢献できる経営を目一杯頑張るだけです。再教育や高齢者への講習、交通安全への貢献なども有力なコンテンツになるはずです。一方で、教習所のビジネスの中で培ってきた企業文化やブランドは、決して自動車教習だけにしか使えないものではないと思うのです」
　地域とのつながりが深まるほど、ヒントに触れる機会も広がっていく。限られたパイを奪い合うのではなく、社員の意識改革とお客様の感動を追求、地域社会貢献を三位一体で継続し、それにより、市場を切り開いていく。それは介護ビジネスでも、健康ビジネスでも、保育園でもいいはずだ。武蔵境自動車教習所の第一の強みである人財、特にホスピタリティやおもてなしの精神、お客様に寄り添った対応力という点を活かすことで事業を拡大していけるのだ。すでに、2014年より新規事業開発室を新設。また社長自らアメリカ、スタン

Many Things Still to Achieve

Takahashi's future interests are kindled in automatic driving. What exactly does this mean?
"I believe that the development and spread of automatic driving will become a national policy. This will likely take shape in the next five or 10 years. It is not just Japan, the situation is the same in the West. Google are already developing driverless cars, aren't they? While it would be a blow to the driving school industry, this is what the world wants in order to make an even safer car society."

At such a juncture, the curriculum of driving schools could shrink to half or even a third of what it is now. How will he survive?
"To be honest, I'm not so worried. Right now driving schools are my main business, and we are absolutely dedicated to management that creates employment through our own means, as well as contributing to society. Re-education and classes for the elderly, as well as contributing to traffic safety should become important content. On another front, I believe that the corporate culture and brand we have built up inside the driving school business will definitely be applicable in areas outside of the industry."

The more contact with the community deepens, the more chances there are to glean hints. Rather than snatching slices of a limited pie, aim to renew the mindset of employees and to provide excitement to customers while contributing to society – by continuing this holy trinity, it will be possible to trailblaze the market. It could be the caregiving business, the health business, or the kindergarten business. It will be possible to expand the business through drawing on human resources, the principal strength of Musashisakai Driving School, and in particular the spirit of hospitality and engaging with customers in a way that is sensitive to their feelings. Already, Takahashi has newly established a start-up business development office since 2014. On top of this, as representative director and President of the company, has spent time in the U.S. as a visiting researcher at Stanford University, where he is

フォード大学の客員研究員として渡米し、新規事業の開発や事業転換について研究を進めている。さらには「高齢者の方に、より長く健康でクルマを楽しんでいただくために何ができるか」といったことをコンセプトに、現在、異業種とのコラボレーションによりビジネスモデルの構築も進めている。それら共通の想いは社員を幸せにすることである。社員の雇用、活躍の場を確保し、地域からの雇用も促進していく。

　武蔵境という街に行くと、「あらゆること」に対して感動的なサービスが受けられる。笑顔があふれている。武蔵境が近いからそこを利用する、という流れから、すばらしい企業がある武蔵境を選んで住みたい、という人が現れるようにさえなれる。待機児童が少ない自治体や、医療費補助が手厚い自治体には若い家族が集まる。それとまったく同じ話なのだ。国立ではなく武蔵境。府中ではなく武蔵境。自動車教習所がけん引する、おもてなしがあふれる街としてのブランドが構築できれば、武蔵境自動車教習所に惹かれて入社してくる大学生のように、全国から人が集まってくる。

「まだまだ、できることはいっぱいあります」

　そう笑う髙橋の顔は、誰よりも楽しそうだった。

株式会社武蔵境自動車教習所
所在地：〒180-0022　東京都武蔵野市境2-6-43
設立：1960年8月1日
資本金：1100万円
代表者：代表取締役会長　髙橋　勇、代表取締役社長　髙橋明希
事業内容：自動車教習業務（普通車・中型車・普通二輪車・大型二輪車）・高齢者教習・取得時教習・ペーパードライバー教習業務

conducting research into developing new businesses and transformation of business. Furthermore, based on the concept of "what can we do to help elderly people to enjoy driving later on in life healthily," he is pursuing cross-industrial collaboration to construct a business model pursuant to this. These common desires bring happiness to employees. Secure employment for employees, give them a place to shine, and stimulate employment in the area.

If you go to the town of Musashi Sakai, it is possible to receive impressive service for "all things." There are smiles everywhere. There is currently a shift underway - from people making use of Musashi Sakai because it is close - to people deliberately choosing to live there because it has so many excellent companies. Young families flock to municipalities with short waiting lists for pre-school places, and are incentivized to relocate to municipalities which offer generous medical subsidies. It is exactly the same concept. Not Kunitachi but Musashi Sakai. Not Fuchu, but Musashi Sakai. If the town can be branded in terms of a place brimming with hospitality, for which a driving school is providing the torque, people will flock from all over the country akin to university students who have their hearts set on finding employment at Musashisakai Driving School.

"There are still many, many things to do."

Laughing as he says this, Takahashi looks like he is enjoying himself more than anyone else.

Company Profile
Musashisakai Driving School Co., Ltd.
Address: 2-6-43 Sakai, Musashino-shi, Tokyo 180-0022
Established: August 1, 1960
Capital: JPY 11 million
Representative: Isamu Takahashi, Chairman
Aki Takahashi, President
Business Description: Driving Instruction for passenger/mid-sized cars and motorcycles, Driving training for elderly drivers, Provide mandatory training/lecture at license acquisition, Driving training for "no-experienced" drivers.

ジャパン・ブランドの挑戦04

待ちのEMSから、攻めのブランディングカンパニーへ

YURIホールディングス代表取締役、
エーピーアイ代表取締役
須田哲生

**グローバル企業の信頼を受け続けてきた
EMSの優良企業が、なぜ今
「自社ブランド」にこだわりはじめたのか?**

秋田の大企業集団、由利工業グループから生まれた
YURIホールディングス。製造受託企業として
長年グローバルマーケットを戦ってきた技術を活かし、
今新たに「自社ブランドの旗」を建てようとしている。その橋頭堡、
エーピーアイの挑戦を陣頭指揮する須田哲生代表取締役の思いとは?
文中、敬称略

The Ascent of The Japan Brand 04

FROM PASSIVE ELECTRONICS MANUFACTURING SERVICES TO A PROACTIVE BRANDING COMPANY

CEO, API Co.,Ltd.,
CEO, YURI HOLDINGS Co.,Ltd.
Tetsuo Suda

Why has a top EMS company trusted by global corporations now decided to pursue its "own company brand"?

YURI HOLDINGS Co., Ltd. ("YURI HOLDINGS") was spawned by Akita's large corporate YURI Kogyo Group Co., Ltd.
Drawing on technologies built up through many years competing in global markets as a contract manufacturing company, YURI HOLDINGS is now working towards hoisting a flag with its "own company" brand.

押しも押されもせぬ大企業

　秋田県南部、由利地域。「秋田富士」と呼ばれる美しい鳥海山の麓に、この地と世界とを結ぶ、青々とした日本海が広がっている。YURIホールディングスは2015年4月に設立された。由利地域を中心に、長年エレクトロニクスや精密機器等の開発、製造を続け、地域に雇用と活力を生み出してきた由利工業グループのうち、4社の事業会社が集まって構築された持株会社である。

　由利地域は、セラミックコンデンサやHDD用ヘッドなどで世界的なシェアを誇るTDK発祥の地。現在も、同社系企業や、同社が製造を委託している企業の工場、事業所が多数並び、地域の経済的な基盤発展に大きな役割を果たしてきた。由利工業は、ほぼ100% TDKから委託された生産工程を行うEMS（受託生産サービス）企業。創業は1955年というから、すでに60年を超える社歴を有している。YURIホールディングスを構成している4社においても、グループ内外からの委託を受け、金属機械加工や基板実装、機器の組み立て、半導体製造装置、さらに最近では、航空機製造の一部までも担っている。グループの1社、日本SMTを通じてインドネシアとフィリピンにも進出。両国合

秋田県大仙市にあるエーピーアイ本社。廃校になった小学校を社屋として使っている

The head office of API in Daisen-City, Akita Prefecture. A former school is utilized for the company premises.

A Large Corporation with an Established Reputation

The Yuri region, southern Akita Prefecture. At the base of the beautiful Mount Chōkai, known as "Mt.Fuji of Akita," is the lush Sea of Japan linking this area with the world. YURI HOLDINGS was established in April 2015 as a holding company created by the conglomeration of four companies from the YURI Kogyo Group. The group, centered in the Yuri region, has for many years continued to develop and manufacture electronics and precision instruments, creating employment and vitality for the area as a whole.

The Yuri Region is also the birthplace of TDK, which commands a global market share in various domains, including ceramic capacitors and heads for HDDs. To this day, TDK, its group companies and OEMs to which it entrusts manufacturing, all continue to operate many factories and business offices in the region, playing a major role in developing its economic foundation. YURI Kogyo is an EMS (electronics manufacturing company) company carrying out production processes entrusted (almost 100 percent) from TDK. Established in 1955, it has over 60 years history as a company. The four companies that make up YURI HOLDINGS receive commissioned orders from inside and outside the group, handling metal manufacturing and substrate mounting, assemblage of machinery, semiconductor manufacturing equipment and recently, some aircraft manufacture. Through group company NIPPON SMT Co., Ltd., forays are being made into Indonesia and the Philippines, employing a total of 2,000 people in both countries, working in production.

A large company, which has become a household name in the region. However, YURI HOLDINGS leader Tetsuo Suda had come to a decision:

"I want to show the world the fact that our very own brand from this area can be competitive."

Some might feel that Suda's conviction is a case of overreaching or even fretting about the future. I, however, could see new possibilities within Suda's challenge.

わせて2000人もの従業員を確保し、生産に従事している。

　地元では知らぬ人はいない、大企業。しかし、YURIホールディングスを率いる須田哲生には、ある決意があった。

「この地から、自分たちのブランドで勝負できる事実を世界に見せていきたい」

　人によっては、須田の思いは背伸び、あるいは取り越し苦労と感じるかもしれない。だが私は、須田のチャレンジに新たな可能性を見出すのだ。

EMSを取り囲む危機

　まず断っておきたいのだが、YURIホールディングスにおけるEMS事業は、全体として順調である。国際的な優良企業として知られているクライアントから、クオリティの面でも、価格の面でもグローバル市場で勝負できると評価されているからこそ、現在のYURIホールディングスの姿がある。しかし、日本国内におけるEMSの事業環境が決して楽ではないこともまた事実だ。これは一企業の努力や希望によってはどうすることもできない、いわばマクロ的な環境変化の結果だ。

　1990年代以前であれば、日本の製造業にとってライバルはいなかったといえる。あるいは、90年代もそうだったかもしれない。しかし、アジアの新興諸国に加え、ベルリンの壁崩壊に象徴される東西冷戦の終結や、中国の改革開放（社会主義市場経済）が進むにつれ、東欧や中国の安価かつ大量の労働力がグローバル市場に続々と流れ込むことになった。彼らがより高度な付加価値を市場に送り出せるようになればなるほど、日本のモノ作りを支えてきた製造業、とりわけEMSのビジネスモデルには苦しい局面が訪れる。どれだけコストを削り、質の良い製品、遅滞のない製造工程を供給しようと、海外で同じ

The Crisis Engulfing EMS

Just to avoid any confusion, the EMS business of YURI HOLDINGS is solid overall. YURI HOLDINGS remains in the game precisely because its clients who are renowned international companies – consider YURI HOLDINGS to be competitive in the global market in terms of both quality and price. However, it is also a fact that the EMS business environment within Japan is not enjoying smooth sailing. This is the result of a shift in the macro environment, which no company can hope to tackle through effort or ambition.

Prior to the 1990s, it can be said that there were no rivals to Japanese manufacturing. The same could even be said of the 1990s. However, factors including new emerging countries in Asia, the end of the Cold War as symbolized by the bringing down of the Berlin Wall, and the advance of reform and throwing open of China (a socialist market economy) – all conspired to precipitate a torrential flow of cheap and plentiful labor from Eastern Europe and China into global markets. As these workers became able to bring increasingly higher added value into the market, the manufacturing industry and in particular the EMS business model underpinning Japanese manufacturing entered a harsh phase. No matter how hard companies attempted to cut costs and provide high quality products through a punctual manufacturing process, given that the same could be obtained overseas at a fraction of the cost, those earnest efforts alone would not be enough.
"Not just in Taiwan and Korea, but even in China, the quality of staple manufactured articles is no different to that of Japan."

When it came to the manufactured of staple articles that rely on mass-production and scale-merit, Japan could not be on mass competitive quantities, and would lose out. Suda and his cohorts were entertaining these concerns from around 2000. It would not do to attack the corporations on the ordering side. As global corporations, they are doing battle in global markets. What is more, no one could stem the inexorable tide of globalization.

ことが何分の1かのコストでできる以上、努力しただけではどうにもならなくなるのだ。

「台湾、韓国だけでなく、中国でも、汎用品のクオリティは日本と変わりません」

　大量生産型、スケールメリットを活かした汎用品生産では、日本勢は数量で勝負にならず淘汰されてしまう。須田たちの頭の中には、2000年頃から、こうした懸念が広がっていた。発注先の企業を責めることなどできない。グローバル企業である以上、グローバル市場の中で戦っているのだから。そしてもはや世界中の誰にも、グローバル化を止めることなどできはしない。

このままでは悔しい、面白くない！

　こうした中、由利工業を中心とするグループ各社は、高付加価値化や海外進出などで対応してきたといえる。汎用品は海外工場の労働力を活用して価格競争力を担保する一方、国内では他の企業、他の国では作れないモノを開発・受託する、というソリューションだ。そして、それはある程度うまくいっている。数年間隔で直面する厳しい円高局面も、一時はサプライチェーンを寸断した東日本大震災も乗り越え、現在に至っている。しかし、須田は気づいていた。

「努力することは大切です。しかし、今の私たちにはオリジナルのブランドがない。結局、私たちの作るモノは、どこまで行っても価格と品質だけで比較されるのです」

　それでは、モノ作りの集団として悔しいし、面白くない。これは、マクロ的な事情とは別に、須田の心の中に長い間宿っていた気持ちだった。その上、もし今後これまで以上に厳しい経営環境にさらされれば、どれだけ長い歴史と知名度を誇っていようと、そろばんに乗らないという理由で業容が縮小するリスク

| The Ascent of The Japan Brand 04 | API Co., Ltd. | Tetsuo Suda |

This Path Only Leads to Regret and is Not at All Inspiring!

Facing this predicament, YURI Kogyo and its various group companies attempted to stay afloat through offering even higher added value and expanding overseas. For staple articles, while leveraging the labor of overseas factories would secure price competitiveness, domestically the solution would be to develop and receive orders for products that could not be made by other Japanese or foreign corporations. This bore fruit to a certain extent. YURI Kogyo successfully weathered high-yen phases that appear every several years, and also the Great East Japan Earthquake, which temporarily severed the supply chain. However, something had come to Suda's attention: "It is important to make an effort. However, at the moment we do not possess an original brand. Ultimately, products we make will only be compared in terms of their price and quality, no matter how far we go."

For a group involved in manufacturing, this was regretful and uninteresting. This was a feeling that had been welling up in Suda's heart for sometime, and was separate from the macro context. Furthermore, if confronted by a yet harsher operating environment, no amount of boasting about their proud history or name recognition would reduce the risk of their business scope dwindling, due to it no longer making financial sense. Would it not be possible to channel their efforts for higher added value together with original ideas in their own products, which they could appeal to the masses with as their own brands? With this in mind, Suda spent the last ten years researching and developing new businesses leveraging their own brands.

In recent years, quantitative easing policies - referred to as being of "another dimension" - have resulted in a rapidly weakening yen, allowing domestic manufacturing hubs to gradually recover. Such a sense of relief also permeated within the Yuri region and within the group. However, it is exactly now when EMS is in a sound condition that is the time to plant seeds and start planning new moves. Our own raw abilities, our own ideas, our own conceptions. Brand

からは逃れられない。高付加価値化への努力やオリジナルのアイデアを、自分たちの製品として、自分たちのブランドとして、世に問えないか。須田は、そのような思いで、この10年ほどを自社ブランドによる新規事業の研究開発に費やしてきた。

　ここ数年、「異次元」と形容された量的金融緩和策によって急速に円安となり、国内の製造拠点は次第に息を吹き返している。由利地域にも、グループ内にも安堵の雰囲気が広がっている。しかし、EMSが順調な今だからこそ、種をまき、新たな手を打っていきたい。自分たちの実力、自分たちのアイデア、自分たちの想い。そして、それらが形作る、YURIとしてのブランド作り。須田の想いは揺るがない。

エーピーアイという橋頭堡

　2010年、須田は大きな決断をする。グループ内で事業を再編し、そのうちの1社であるエーピーアイを、大量生産型EMSから、産学連携をベースとした開発型企業へシフトさせたのだ。

　エーピーアイは1983年に設立された。もともとはカラーテレビ用偏向ヨーク（ブラウン管に欠かせないコイルの一種）の一貫生産工場だった。以来、電子機器の組み立てを中心として、ナノテクノロジーまで対応できる生産工場として機能していた。一方で2005年から、地元秋田の研究機関と連携した共同研究開発も担っていた。2010年は、円高の進行と新興諸国のキャッチアップによって、製造業の海外移転が直近のピークに達していた。そこでEMSの機能をグループの他社に移転した上で、エーピーアイを純粋な開発型企業として再スタートさせることにしたのだ。当然、人員体制は大幅にスリムになる。

building as YURI to give form to these. Suda's conviction was unwavering.

API, The Bridgehead

In 2010, Suda came to a major decision. He would realign businesses within the group, and shift one of these companies, API, from a mass-production type EMS to a development-type enterprise based on academic-industrial alliances.

API was established in 1983. It started out as an integrated production plant for deflection yokes (a type of coil indispensable for cathode-ray tubes) for color televisions. Since then, it has functioned as a production plant focused on assembling electronic equipment, and also capable of handling nanotechnology. On another front, it also entered an R&D tie-up from 2005 with a local Akita research organization. In 2010, the shift of manufacturing industry overseas reached its most recent peak, due to the appreciating yen and catch-up progress by emerging nations. At that point, Suda decided to transfer the EMS function to other companies within the group, and relaunch API purely as a development-type company. Needless to say, the staff organization was significantly slimmed down. Former factories were sold, and an invitation came from Daisen City (famous for the Omagari National Fireworks Competition) to use a closed-down school as factory premises; Suda accepted the invitation and moved in.

The role of bridgehead, so to speak, for constructing the YURI brand that Suda dreamed of was now to be taken up by API. It would constitute a hub for creating products that customers would select not just on the basis of cost-performance but because of the value inherent in YURI ideas and the YURI brand. It would be the place where principally up-and-coming elite employees would plant seeds looking 10 or 20 years into the future.

Suda, who would concurrently serve as API representative explains:
"This is not a place where we take orders about what to make. This is where

旧工場は売却、「大曲の花火」で知られる大仙市から、廃校になった小学校を社屋に使用しないかという誘いを受け、移転することになった。

いわば、須田の夢見るYURIブランド構築のための、橋頭堡。それが新しくエーピーアイが担うことになった役割だ。コストパフォーマンスだけでなく、YURIのアイデア、YURIのブランドによって選ばれるモノ作りの拠点。若手を中心に、精鋭社員が10年、20年先への種をまく場所。

自らエーピーアイの代表を兼務する須田は言う。

「ここは、言われたモノを作る場所ではありません。私たちがワクワクしながら作りたいモノを作る場なのです」

そして須田は、秋田で、日本の地方で戦う意味をも見出し始めていた。エーピーアイは、地元の希望の星でもあるのだ。

画期的チャレンジ「わたりジョーズ君」

2005年、須田のもとに、今日に至るきっかけとなるオファーがやってきた。地元、秋田大学工学資源学部からの共同研究開発の誘いだった。現在、ほぼ全国の警察本部等で採用されるに至った、歩行環境シミュレータ「わたりジョーズ君」。自動車運転用ではなく、体験者が歩行者として自動車の走る道路を疑似的に横断しながら、危険性の発見や改善の手がかりを発見できる、世界初の歩行者用シミュレータだ。

秋田県は、2014年時点で全人口のほぼ3分の1が高齢者という、高齢化率トップ地域としても知られている。高齢者が交通事故に巻き込まれる要因として、自らの知覚や運動能力の衰えを正確に認識できず、結果として危険な横断をしてしまうことがある。自らの横断がどのくらい危険なのか、本人が簡単

we can get excited about making the products that we want to."

Thus, Suda began to uncover the significance of leading the charge from Akita, in rural Japan. API was to be the local area's star of hope.

"*Watari Jozu Kun*" – a Groundbreaking Challenge

In 2005, Suda received an offer that would lead him to where he is today. It was an invitation to take part in joint research and development with Akita University Faculty of Engineering and Resources Sciences a local entity. Currently, nearly all police headquarters throughout Japan have adopted the Walking Environment Simulator "*Watari Jozu Kun*." Not designed for car drivers, this is the world's first pedestrian-use simulator, and allows users to undergo a mock experience of crossing a busy road, helping them to detect dangers and providing clues for improving their road-crossing ability.

As of 2014, Akita Prefecture is known as a region with the aged population, with elderly people constituting one third of its citizens. One cause of elderly people becoming involved in traffic accidents is their inability to accurately perceive their deteriorating perception and exercise capacities, resulting in dangerous road crossing. Could a method be developed allowing individuals to easily comprehend just how dangerous their road crossing was? Such a notion occurred to Professor Kazutaka Mitobe of Akita University. It was API that was nominated as partner for the joint research and development.

There were certain steps required for making this simulator a reality. First and foremost was the job of creating computer graphics that would be displayed on screens in front of and to the left and right of the user, in order to recreate real road crossing conditions: The more realistic the better. Another key step was to create sensors to go around the user's head and feet in order to read their movements. Both of these steps were made possible thanks to the knowledge and manufacturing prowess built up by the YURI Kogyo Group in the EMS business over the years. 2007 was the year that this vision

に把握する方法を提供できないか。それが、秋田大学の水戸部一孝教授の思いだった。その共同研究、開発の相手として指名されたのが、エーピーアイだった。このシミュレータを実現するにはステップがある。まずリアルな道路横断の状況を再現するため、体験者の前方と左右のスクリーンに表示するコンピュータグラフィクスを作成すること。リアルであればあるほどいい。もうひとつは、体験者の足元や頭部で本人の動きを読み取るセンサである。いずれもEMSのビジネスにおいて培った由利工業グループの知見と製造力によって実現することができた。2007年に商品化にこぎつけ、大分県警察本部に初出荷を果たしている。これは、グループ企業にとって画期的な出来事だったといえるだろう。自社のブランドで開発した新製品の発売、そして自社が息づく地域の問題解決のために絞ったアイデアの結実。さらに、今後の業容変容の可能性と、雇用確保、増大への希望。こうして、須田たちのチャレンジに新しい一歩が刻まれた。

ヘルスケアビジネスの可能性

歩行環境シミュレータ「わたりジョーズ君」は、一言で言えばヘルスケア関連商品ということになる。それまで由利工業グループが取り組んでこなかったジャンルだ。須田たちは、初めからヘルスケア分野への参入を思い描いていたわけではなかった。だが、高齢化という地域の課題への解決策を日々考えていた地元研究機関とのコラボレーションが、グループ全体で"地域社会への貢献"という理念を掲げる須田たちにとって、新たな貢献の道を気づかせることとなった。秋田県が他県に、そして世界に先駆けて経験している超・高齢化社会を、日本の他の地域も、そして東アジアをはじめとする海外各国も、こ

became a product, with the first shipment going to Oita Prefectural Police Headquarters. This could be said to constitute an epoch-making achievement for the group companies. The launching of new products developed through their own company's brand, and the coming to fruition of ideas narrowed down in order to resolve issues in the very region where their company exists. Furthermore, the possibilities transformed their future scope of business, secured employment and hopes for increasing it. This marked a new step for Suda and his cohorts in rising to their challenge.

Possibilities in the Healthcare Business

The *"Watari Jozu Kun"* walking environment simulator essentially comes under the category of healthcare-related product. It was a genre unexplored by the YURI Kogyo Group up until then. Suda and his team had not initially intended to make an entry into the healthcare sector. However, it was collaboration with local research institutions working on a daily basis toward solutions to the regional issue of an aging population that provided the signpost to a new way of making a contribution for Suda and his team - who were united under the group-wide mission of "contributing to the local society." Akita is ahead of other prefectures, and indeed the world, in confronting the issue of an ultra-aging population. Other regions in Japan

秋田大学との共同研究開発によって製品化された、歩行環境シミュレータ「わたりジョーズ君」
The *"Watari Jozu Kun"* Walking Environment Simulator, made into a commercial reality through joint R&D with Akita University.

れから後追いで確実に体験する。自分たちの持つ技術力や開発力が、地元・秋田の"社会課題"の解決に役立ち、ひいては秋田から日本全国、そして世界に貢献することができるのだ。

　問題は高齢化だけではない。秋田県の人口は、年間1万5000人近く減少するという。県の人口が103万人だから1％減少していることになる。減少率は全国一だ。その背景には、働く世代の人口が流出していることがある。結果、14歳以下の子どもは全体の1割強しかおらず、これも全国最小だという。雇用がないからふるさとを離れざるを得ない。そのため子どもも増えず、高齢者だけが残る。須田は、高齢化県秋田で生きる意味を、秋田でできることをしながら、秋田県の雇用を増やしていくことに見出している。

「秋田にこだわっている、という気持ちは間違いなくあります。この地だからこそできること、そして秋田に戻りたくなるような、積極的に来たくなるような面白いことをしたい。この地で行く末を案じている人なら、誰もがその思いを持っていると思います」

　地域に貢献することが、地域の発展を促す。ヘルスケアは、そのフックとなり得るものなのだ。

はずむ研究開発

　グループ各社が手がけてきた技術、特にモーションキャプチャを含むセンサ技術は、ヘルスケアや予防医療への親和性が高い。今後マーケットの拡大が期待されるだけでなく、ニッチなジャンルも多数生まれやすい。

　「わたりジョーズ君」はほぼ「全国制覇」を成し遂げ、警察だけでなく自動車教習所などの講習にも取り上げられつつある。やはり少子高齢化で顧客が

and countries around the world including those in East Asia will soon be experiencing the same problem themselves. Suda and his team's very own technological prowess and capacity to develop will be instrumental in resolving Akita's "social issues" in their own backyard – and can then contribute to the rest of Japan and then the world.

An aging population is not the only issue. Apparently, Akita Prefecture's population is decreasing to the tune of nearly 15,000 people per year. Given that the population of the prefecture is 1.03 million people, this amounts to a percent decrease. Such a diminution rate is the highest in the country. In the background to this is the fact that the working-age population is flowing outwards. As a result, children under 14 years old make up just over 10 percent of the overall total, the lowest ratio in the country. Lacking employment, people have no choice but to leave their hometown. This means that the number of children does not increase, inevitably leading to an aging demographic. Suda considers the significance of living in the increasingly graying Akita Prefecture to be increasing employment in the prefecture.

"It is true to say that I am dedicated to Akita. I want to do something interesting that is only possible in this area, something conducive to making people want to proactively return to Akita. I think that anybody worried about the fate of this region would share that feeling."

Contributing to the region encourages regional development. Healthcare has the potential to become the hook for this.

Effervescent R&D

Technology pioneered by group companies, in particular sensor technology including motion capture, is highly compatible with healthcare and preventative medicine. The market is expected to expand in future, as well as spawning many niche genres.

"*Watari Jozu Kun*" has pretty much conquered the nation, and is used not

減り、業績の厳しい教習所業界に、新しい需要を呼び起こすアイテムとなりつつある。

エーピーアイでは、引き続き他のアプローチによるヘルスケア分野の研究、開発が進んでいる。2009年には秋田県立脳血管研究センターとの共同開発がスタートした。テーマは、手術室などで床に落ちた手術針を探す探知機の開発である。手術用の縫合針の中には、技術の進展によって目視が困難なほどにまで細くなっている「マイクロ針」などがあるが、使用した針の本数は逐次確認し、落とした針は確実に回収しなければならない。万が一患者の体内に残っている場合、そのまま縫合すると重大な医療事故に結びついてしまう。そこで、術前、術中、そして術後と、3段階にわたってチェックをかけることが一般的だ。かつてはそれほど難しい作業ではなかったが、現在では大げさではなく、床に這いつくばるようにしてライトを当てて検索しなければならない。針の進歩によって患者には恩恵が生まれた反面、現場には時間、労力ともに重い負担となっていた。4年の歳月をかけて独自のアルゴリズムの研究開発を重ねた結果、2013年、2ミリ以上の縫合針に対応できるコンパクトな手術針探知機「ニードルハンター」として商品化された。医療現場からは、今まで解決できなかったニッチなニーズを満たしてくれる商品との好感触を得ているという。

世界中の視覚障がい者への福音

また、秋田県立大学とのコラボレーションは、視覚障がい者への画期的なアイテムとして結実した（開発当時は、グループ企業秋田精工が担当）。

「スマート電子白杖（はくじょう）」。名前の通り、見た目は視覚障がい者用の「白い杖」。しかしグリップ部分にセンサが内蔵されていて、正面と上方の障害物を検知し、

just by the police but also increasingly as part of training provided by driving schools. Inevitably, as customers decrease due to the falling birth rate, driving schools facing the pinch are adopting it as a new item capable of awakening untapped demand.

API is promoting research and development in health care sectors leveraging other approaches. 2009 saw the launch of joint development with the Akita Research Institute for Brain and Blood Vessels. The theme was to develop a detection machine for locating operating needles dropped onto the floor of the operating theater.

Due to the progression of technology, within needles used for surgery are "micro needles" that are almost invisible to the naked eye; operating theaters have to constantly ascertain the number of needles used and must recoup any needles that have been inadvertently dropped onto the floor. If a needle were accidently left inside the body of a patient and sewn up inside them, it could result in a major medical incident. Given this, it is standard practice to conduct a three-part check before, during, and after surgery. While this was traditionally not a particularly troublesome task, at present it is actually the case that people have to crawl around on the floor with a torch looking for dropped needles. While progress in needles has brought considerable benefits for patients, on the other hand it has greatly burdened doctors and medical staff working in the operating theater in terms of energy expended and time. Four long years spent researching and developing a proprietary algorithm bore fruit in 2013 with the product launch of the "NEEDLE HUNTER" compact surgical needle detector, capable of locating surgical needles bigger than 2mm. From the front line of medical care, it is already receiving a glowing response as a product that satisfies a niche need that was hitherto unresolved.

Good News for Visually Impaired People Around the World

On another front, collaboration with Akita Prefectural University bore fruit in

振動で知らせてくれる。視覚障がい者にとって、ひとりで自由に外出することはQOL（生活の質）向上のために不可欠だ。通常は一般の白杖や盲導犬を使用することになるが、実はこれらではわからない障害物が多数存在するのだという。とりわけ、正面や上方に迫っている物体、たとえばトラックの荷台からはみ出している積み荷や歩道にせり出している木の枝、看板などは避けがたく、大きなストレスとなっていた。そこに、秋田県立大学が開発した超音波センサを活用した検出システムと、由利工業グループが培ってきた製造技術、耐久性がインテグレートされ、新商品の誕生に至った。海外製の同種の杖がこれまで10万〜25万円程度していたのに対して、3万〜4万円台と圧倒的なコストパフォーマンスを実現。かつ一般の白杖とほぼ変わらないほどの軽量化まで果たしている。

　視覚障がい者の数は、秋田県内では数千人。しかし全国では30万人以上、全世界では3億人近く存在しているといわれる。事故を未然に防ぎ、社会参加や個々の夢の実現に貢献しながら、新しいビジネスを切り開けるはずだ。

　一方、ユニークなシーズも生まれてきている。「フットプラネタリウム」と名づけられた商品は、足裏のいわゆる「ツボ」が、プラネタリウムの星のように表

視覚障がい者にストレスなく外出してほしいという願いから生まれた「スマート電子白杖」
The "Smart Electronics White Cane," born from the hope of empowering the visually impaired to walk around unhindered.

the form of a groundbreaking item for visually impaired persons, the "Smart Electric White Cane" (group company Akita Seiko Co., Ltd. was in charge during the development phase).

As the name suggests, this invention resembles the "White Cane" used by the visually impaired. However, the grip is mounted with sensors. allowing users to identify obstacles above and in front of them, communicated via vibrations. For the visually impaired, being able to step outside by themselves is indispensable for quality of life. There are actually many obstacles that the conventional white canes and guide dogs are unable to detect. In particular, the visually impaired have found it difficult to avoid hanging objects directly in front or above - such as cargo jutting out from the load-carrying trays of trucks, tree branches jutting out into the pavement, and billboards – all a major cause of stress. A detection system using an ultrasonic sensor developed by Akita Prefectural University was integrated with the manufacturing technology and durability built up by YURI Kogyo Group, leading to the birth of a new product. As opposed to the 100,000-250,000 yen price tag attached to similar canes manufactured abroad, the Smart Electric White Cane priced in the 30,000 - 40,000 yen range offers overwhelming price performance. On top of this, it hardly differs from conventional White Canes in terms of weight.

There are several thousand visually impaired people in Akita Prefecture. This number rises to over 300,000 people in Japan, and nearly 300 million people worldwide. While contributing to preventing accidents and enabling social participation and the fulfillment of individual dreams, this technology promises to be a trailblazer for new businesses.

In other areas, new seeds are emerging. A product called "Foot Planetarium" displays the so-called "pressure points" from the underside of the foot in a configuration akin to stars in a planetarium, allowing a person receiving a foot massage to communicate to the practitioner where they want massaged through light and sound, without the need for conversation. <u>It was developed in collaboration with Nursing Consultants Ltd. (President Muramatsu Seiko),</u>

示され、施術される人が施術者に対して、どこを押してほしいのか会話をせずに音と光で伝えることができる。訪問看護業界のスペシャリストである看護コンサルタント株式会社(代表取締役 村松静子)とのコラボで開発した、いわば、最前線での非言語コミュニケーションツール。今後は介護や福祉の現場に応用できる商品開発を続けていくという。

ブランディングは社会問題解決につながる

　高齢化県の悩みに向き合い、その解決に向けてスタートしたヘルスケアという新たな分野への進出。しかも自社ブランドによる新規ビジネスの開拓によって、エーピーアイ、そしてYURIホールディングスには新しい取引関係が多数生まれた。歩行環境シミュレータ「わたりジョーズ君」は、2013年に警察庁の「高齢者の交通安全教育のためのシニアリーダー育成モデル事業」に採用されたことがきっかけで大きく伸びた。これは、高齢者からリーダーを募って他の高齢者に交通安全の指導を行うというもの。まさにいち早く世相の流れに乗れた好例だろう。順調に進む納品と並行して改良を重ね、2015年からは「新わたりジョーズ君」へモデルチェンジした。CGソフトの改良が図られ、3Dゲームで使用されている開発環境を使ってよりリアルな状況の描写が可能になった。特に、雨や雷の質感が鮮明になったという。センサも完全自社開発製品に切り替え、コストを削減した。

　また、かつてセットで200キロあった重量が100キロ以上軽量化され、可搬性が増した。各種イベント会場などに持ち込んで体験してもらう用途がメインのため、現場からは好評を得ているという。高齢者や自動車教習所に加え、最近は小学校などの交通安全教育にも使用されるようになった。特に交通事故

a specialist in visit nursing industry, suffice to say, this is the frontline of non-verbal communication tools. There is every intention to continue developing products that can be utilized by those working at the coalface of nursing and welfare.

Branding Helps to Resolve Social Issues

Facing up to the concerns of a prefecture with an aging population, YURI HOLDINGS advanced into the new area of healthcare to start working towards solutions. Pioneering a new business through their own brand, meanwhile, spawned many new business relationships for API and YURI HOLDINGS. A major catalyst propelling the growth of road crossing simulator "*Watari Jozu Kun*" came in 2013 when it was adopted by the National Police Agency as a "Model Business for Nurturing Senior Leaders for Traffic Safety Education for the Elderly." This involves recruiting leaders from among elderly people to provide leadership to other senior citizens regarding road safety; a good example of being quick off the mark to tune into the true state of society. Following steady delivery and ongoing improvements, in 2015 the model was upgraded to "New *Watari Jozu Kun*." With improved CG software, this upgrade provides even more realistic conditions by utilizing the development environment used in 3D games. In particular, the rain and lightning sensation is clearer. Costs have also been curtailed by switching to sensors completely developed and manufactured inhouse.

Also, the weight of the whole set was reduced by half, from 200 kg to 100kg, making it even more portable. Its main usage is at events and other venues where people can try out the experience, and is proving very popular.

As well as for the elderly and driving schools, recently it has been adopted by elementary schools for traffic safety education. A lot of these are in prefectures and regions with a notably high amount of traffic accidents.

"While there is still a long way to go, I feel very happy and encouraged that our

の多い県や地方で採用されることが多いという。

「まだまだこれからの部分も多いのですが、今まででは考えられないような場所に、自社の技術、製品が届いていることがうれしいし、心強いです」

こういった取り組みを通して、社会の直面している問題への啓蒙や、解決への貢献という自分たちの想いが、徐々に伝え広まっていることに、須田は確かな手応えを感じ始めている。

ブランディングとは、点をつなぐ意志を持つこと

須田がときどき思い起こす言葉がある。アップルの創業者、故スティーブ・ジョブズの「コネクティング・ザ・ドッツ」。点をつないでいけば、それがやがて線となり、今からは想像もできない将来につながっていく——。YURIホールディングスや由利工業グループの実力、実績は、恐らく個々の「点」としては申し分のないクオリティである。しかし、もしEMSに徹していたら、世界に対して見せるような線を引く機会は、恐らく永遠になかっただろう。

「今まで私たちは、受注したモノをスペック通りに作ってきた。それ自体はすば

「創造によって地域社会に貢献する」という企業理念のもと、日々モノ作りに励む社員たち。
In line with the company philosophy of "contributing to the local community through creation," employees spend every day devoted to creating products.

technology and products are being used in places that we never would have thought possible."

Through such initiatives, Suda is beginning to feel a definite response to the fact that the desire to contribute towards raising awareness and solving issues faced by society is gradually resonating further afield.

Branding Means Having the Will to Connect the Dots

Suda recalls a certain motto from time to time. It is that of the late Steve Jobs, founder of Apple: "Connecting the dots." If you connect the dots, they will eventually form a line, leading into a future beyond what you can imagine. The raw ability and track record of YURI HOLDINGS and YURI Kogyo Group Co. Ltd. are of unquestionable quality in terms of each individual "dot." However, if they had devoted themselves to EMS, there would probably have never been any opportunities to draw a line worthy of showing to the world. "Up until now, we received orders to manufacture products in line with specifications. This in itself was a wonderful thing. However, in order to inject our true capabilities into cool innovations, I believe that we definitely need the strong desire to etch our own line."

Now, if they could change, big chances would materialize. Business will grow beyond all imagination, the coolness of YURI will be admired, and one day brand value will come to exist within a corporate philosphy that is not judged solely on price and quality.

Suda cannot hide his desire to leverage the company's own brand to expand overseas.
"At a business convention in Tawian, "*Watari Jozu Kun*," "NEEDLE HUNTER" and "Smart Electric White Cane" were all amazingly well received. We will continuously monitor reactions in global markets."

The onset of an aging population is not a problem limited to Japan, and will in the near future come to bear upon Taiwan, Korea and China with its

らしいことです。ただ、私たちの本来の力をクールなイノベーションにつなげていくには、自ら線をつなごうとする強い意志が絶対に必要だと思うのです」

今、変えることができれば、大きなチャンスが開けていく。想像もしない大きなビジネスが広がり、YURIのクールさが賞賛され、決して価格と品質だけで判断されない「想い」にブランド価値が生まれる日がやってくるはずだ。

須田は、自社ブランドによる海外進出への想いも隠さない。

「台湾での商談会では、『わたりジョーズ君』をはじめ、『ニードルハンター』、『スマート電子白杖』への反応も上々でした。今後も継続的に世界市場での反応をモニターしていきます」

高齢化の進展は日本だけの課題ではなく、台湾、韓国、そして巨大な内需を抱える中国にも近い将来確実にやってくる。ゆくゆくは、国民皆保険制度が整っていない欧米での新サービス、新市場開拓も視野に入れる。これは、同じ「海外進出」という言葉でも、インドネシアやフィリピンに生産現場を移したソリューションとは根本的、本質的に異なる性格を持つことは言うまでもない。今、まいているブランディングの種が、やがて世界で花開く日も遠くはないはずだ。

ファーストコールカンパニーであり続ける

須田には、もうひとつの強い思いがある。

「この地域における、『ファーストコールカンパニー(※)』であり続けることです。エーピーアイならどんなことでもできる、YURIホールディングスなら世界に負けないクオリティで勝負できるという旗を立て続けたいのです」

思えば、秋田の各種研究機関から須田に声がかかったのは、由利工業グループの圧倒的な存在感に加え、須田たちの"チャレンジするという志"を買

(※) ファーストコールカンパニーはタナベ経営の登録商標です。

enormous domestic demand. Someday, there will be opportunities to cultivate new markets and new services in the West, where some countries lack a universal medical insurance system. Needless to say, the same phrase of "overseas expansion" has a completely different nature and meaning to the solution of moving factories over to Indonesia and the Philippines. The day is not far off when branding seeds being planted now will blossom around the world.

Remaining the First Port of Call for Customers

Suda has another strong conviction:
"We want to remain a "first-call company(※)" in this region. We want to continue hoisting a flag that says that API can do anything and that YURI HOLDINGS can triumph through quality that is globally competitive and world-beating."

Looking back, the various research institutions in Akita approached Suda because of the overwhelming and impressive presence of YURI Kogyo Group, but also because they unmistakably endorsed Suda and his team's "desire to take on a challenge." First of all, in his hometown of Akita; before long, from around Japan, and then from around the world. If you want to transform interesting ideas into tangible form, it is important to continue to be regarded by customers as their preferred vendor the company they go to first of.
"Although easily accessed by air from Tokyo, Akita is very rural. It is a somewhat closed society. However, there was the major merit of being able to engage with people from all sorts of backgrounds."

The corporate principle that continues today within the YURI Kogyo Group and YURI HOLDINGS is "contribute to the local society through creation."

YURI HOLDINGS, and within it API, as a testing ground capable of responding flexibly to anything, and as an engine that can convert academic and research knowledge into something that contributes to society, will fulfill the role of sublimating the raw abilities of the entire group into the brand. This,

(※) "First-Call-Company" is the registered trademark of Tanabe Management Consulting Co.,Ltd.

ってくれたからに違いない。まずはふるさと秋田で。やがては日本中、世界中から。面白いアイデアを形にしてくれるなら、最初に電話する企業として認識され続けることが大切だ。

「東京から飛行機で来られるとはいえ、秋田は田舎です。世間も狭い。でもそのおかげでいろいろな立場の方々とつながれる大きなメリットがあります」

由利工業グループ、そしてYURIホールディングスに引き継がれている企業理念は、「創造によって地域社会に貢献する」というものだ。

YURIホールディングス、中でもエーピーアイは、どんなことにも柔軟に対応できる実験の場として、学問や研究の知見を社会貢献の形に変換していくエンジンとして、グループ全体の実力をブランドに昇華する役割を担っていく。ただ、須田の夢はこれだけではない。

「皆様とのご縁も大切にしながら、待つだけの体制から脱却しなければいけません。いずれ完全自社オリジナルの研究開発にまで高めていきたい。『たまたま』持ち込まれた話でうまく行っただけ、と言われるのは悔しいですよ」

YURIの作るモノは面白い、YURIは次にどんなモノを出してくるのか？ 世界からそんな眼差しを浴びる日が、ひとつのゴールになるのだろう。

ブランディングとは、旗を立てることだ

須田の表情には、悲壮感がない。あえて言うなら、さまざまに絡み合ったテーマに対して、健全な危機感と将来への期待感がとてもバランスよく同居しているように見える。EMSからの脱却。自社製品の確立。地域の課題解決、雇用確保と活性化。広く日本、世界に貢献する社会性。そして、ビジネスとしての可能性と持続性。須田に揺るぎがないのは、こうした一見バラバラに

however, is not Suda's only dream.

"While we will always prioritize our many personal relationships, we have to break away from a passive framework where we are always waiting. I want to raise our game up to a level where we pursue original research and development completely in-house. It would be most regretful to be told that we only succeeded because of something that 'happened to come in' from the outside."

YURI makes wonderful products - what will be their next creation? There is hope that a day will come where people around the world regard them in this manner.

Branding is all About Hosting up a Flag

Suda's facial expression is not tinged with any pessimism. Suffice to say, he gives off the impression of a good balance of a healthy sense of crisis and sense of expectation towards the future, with regard to various themes that are intertwined with each other. Breaking away from EMS. Establishing own-company products. Resolving regional issues, securing and revitalizing employment. A social disposition to make an extensive contribution to Japan and to the world. Furthermore, the possibilities for his business and its continuance. Suda's unshakeable attitude is attributable to his conviction to achieve a breakthrough, by way of "branding up" these various themes that appear to be unrelated at first glance, and which are all complicated in their own right.

"If YURI becomes a brand, young people will stop draining outward from Akita, and conversely, people who want to work for YURI will flock to Akita. Such a challenge can absolutely not be met if branding is not successful. Fortunately, we enjoy a stong presence in this region; on the other side of this coin is a sense of responsibility. We will continue to fully respond to the needs of EMS while bringing our own brand into a tangible form,"

見える、そして個別でも難しいテーマを、「ブランディングしていくこと」によってブレイクスルーしようと確信しているからなのではないだろうか。

「YURIがブランドになれば、若い人が秋田から出て行かなくなるし、YURIで働きたいという人が秋田にやってくるようになる。こうしたチャレンジは、ブランディングに成功しない限り絶対にあり得ません。幸い、私たちにはこの地域における存在感があります。それは、責任感と背中合わせでもあります。今後もEMSのニーズにはしっかりと応えていきながら、私たちのブランドを形作る挑戦を続けていきます」

須田の理想は、「秋田は田舎だから……」という言い訳を一掃することだ。

「アメリカに行けば、田舎なのに堂々と世界に向けて発信し続けている地域がたくさんあります。田舎だから何もできない、田舎だから保守的に待っているだけというのは、合理性がないし、言い訳にできません」

YURIホールディングス、由利工業グループ、あるいは由利地域でも秋田県でも、日本の地方でもいい。実はあらゆる課題は、あたかもドミノの牌のように隣り合っているだけなのだ。マインドを変革し、外の社会に認められる形で発信しなければ、自分たちの本来持っている価値ですら伝わらない。地元・秋田への想い、そして社会課題に自らの技術力や開発力を活かし、解決へと導く「貢献」への想いをブランドにまで高めていく。須田は、今日も旗を振り続ける。

エーピーアイ株式会社
所在地：〒019-2401　秋田県大仙市協和船岡字上中野126-1
設立：1983年11月4日
資本金：8000万円
代表者：代表取締役　須田　哲生
事業内容：産学連携を柱とした自社製品開発・販売

Suda would ideally like to get rid of the excuse that "because Akita is in the countryside" once and for all.

"If you go to America, there are many rural regions that manage perfectly well in consistently reaching out to the world. It is illogical to say that being located in the countryside is a hindrance or that the countryside will just be waiting conservatively – it is simply no excuse."

It could be YURI HOLDINGS, YURI Kogyo Group, or in fact the Yuri region, Akita Prefecture, or another region in Japan. The reality is that all issues are actually connected to each other much like domino tiles. Unless you revamp your way of thinking and send out a signal in a manner that society at large will acknowledge, you cannot hope to communicate your inherent value. Commandeering the group's technological and development capabilities, Suda will imbue the brand with affection for his hometown, Akita, as well as the desire to "contribute" toward resolving social issues. Suda continues to hoist up the flag to this day.

Company Profile:
API Co., Ltd.
Address: 126-1 Kaminakano Funaoka Kyowa, Daisen-shi, Akita
Established: November 4, 1983
Capital: JPY 80 million
Representative: Tetsuo Suda, CEO
Business Description: The research and development by industry-university cooperation.

ジャパン・ブランドの挑戦05

ブランドが人材を呼び、人材がブランドを高めていく好循環

関家具　専務
関　正

1台4000万円の一枚板テーブルを売る関家具。
そのブランド構築の背景には、
社員のアイデアを引き出す秘密があった。

「家具の大川」から、1代、47年で370人以上の企業に成長した関家具。
内外のブランドを発掘する家具卸だけでなく、自ら企画、
生産・製作した家具を販売するメーカー商社へと飛躍している。
ブランドが人を呼び、人がブランドを高めている関家具が、
これから目指していくものとは？　関正専務が語る好循環の秘密と夢。
文中、敬称略

The Ascent of The Japan Brand 05

A 'VIRTUOUS CYCLE' THAT PULLS IN TALENTED WORKERS WHO ELEVATE THE BRAND

Executive Director, SEKI FURNITURE Co., Ltd.
Tadashi Seki

Seki Furniture sells tables fashioned from one single plank of timber tables costing 40 million yen each. Underlying the construction of this brand is a secret ability to draw out the ideas of employees.

From "Furniture of Okawa," in 47 years and still under the original founder, SEKI FURNITURE has grown into a company with over 370 employees. As well as discovering and wholesaling furniture brands from Japan and abroad, Seki has grown into a manufacturer-trading firm, handling the design, production and manifacture of its own furniture. SEKI FURNITURE is a company where the brand attracts people, who then make the brand even better. Where do they aim to go from here? Managing Director Tadashi Seki explains the secret of the virtuous cycle and shares his dreams.

平均年齢30歳以下で築くブランド

　福岡県大川市。日本一の家具製造の街として全国的に知られているこの地に、約50年前、流通の革命を起こした男がいた。たったひとり、トラック1台で始まった関家具は、それから47年後、370人を超える、志を同じくする仲間が集う企業となった。眼利きとして発掘した家具だけでなく、自社で企画から生産・製作・卸・販売まで一貫して行い、世界中のマーケットに挑戦するメーカー商社としての動きを一段と強化している。その原動力となっているのは、関家具のブランドに惹かれて入社してきた、新しい世代の社員たちだ。

　創業者の子息で、ブランディングの最前線に立っている専務の関正は、まだ42歳。

「社員の平均年齢は30歳を切っているはずです。勢いがあるのは大変いいのですが、私でも『ご老体』扱いされてしまうのは、ちょっと勘弁してほしい……」

　その笑顔の向こうには、築き上げつつある自社ブランドへの手応えと、今後の家具業界、そしてその向こう側を見つめる強い意志が窺える。

「とにかく自由な社風であることが、若い社員を呼び寄せていると思うんです」

　関はそう語るが、これは決して一朝一夕でできることではない。若い才能、情熱を認め、信じ、引き出して実際にビジネスに落とし込み、しかも成功させているのだから。人を感動させ、仲間を呼び寄せるブランド作りと、呼び寄せられた人がさらにブランド価値を高めるという背中合わせの相乗効果。ブランディングを活力に変換している関家具には、どんな秘密があるのだろうか。そして、日本で、世界で、どう戦っていくのだろうか。

A Brand Created by a Workforce Where the Average Age is Below 30

Okawa City, Fukuoka Prefecture. About 50 years ago, in this area, which is renowned throughout Japan for manufacturing the finest furniture, was a man who started a distribution revolution in the sector. SEKI FURNITURE, which started from one man with one truck, has grown in the 47 years since then into a company of over 370 like-minded individuals. As well as selling furniture hand-picked by its connoisseurs, SEKI FURNITURE handles the entire process spanning production and manufacture through to wholesale and retail, increasingly becoming a manufacturer-trading firm capable of taking on the global market. The driving force behind this comes from the new generation of employees who are extremely fond of the SEKI FURNITURE brand.

Son of the founder, and at the front line of branding, executive director Tadashi Seki is a young 42 years old.

"The average age of my employees is just under 30. It is wonderful to have such youthful vigor, but I do wish people would stop treating me as an old guy..."

Beyond this jovial expression, one can get a glimpse at the response to the company's brand that is still in the process of being built, and the strong determination that is firmly focused on the future of the furniture industry and beyond.

"I think that generally speaking, the company climate of freedom attracts young employees."

Seki makes light of this, but it was certainly not achieved in a short space of time. He has managed to accept and believe in young genius and passion, and succeeding in drawing them out and channeling them into the business. This is a back-to-back synergy based on creating brands that excite people and draw like-minded people together, who then go onto raise the brand value up even higher. What is the secret that enables SEKI FURNITURE to convert branding into vitality? Also, how will they continue their ascent in Japan and around the world?

1台のトラックと父

　1968（昭和43）年。関の父、現社長の関文彦は、家具を満載したトラックを走らせていた。関の祖父、つまり文彦の父はからくり箪笥、食器棚など、箱物家具を製造する職人だったが、父は小売業で修業したのち、独立して卸を始めた。これが関家具の原点であり、今も基幹の事業となっている。関の幼い頃の記憶には、奮闘する父親の姿がはっきりと刻まれている。

「朝、トラック1台で製造業者へ仕入れに向かいます。そしてその足で小売店に売りに行き、その日のうちに現金化して夜には製造元に支払いまで行う。その繰り返しでした」

　当時の家具業界では、革命的とさえいえる画期的な商法だった。家具は流通経路が複雑で、しかも単価が高いだけに現金化に時間がかかることが常だった。少額・長期手形の横行による、決済のルーズさが目立つというのが大川家具業界の通念でさえあった。関の父は、そこに風穴を開けた。自らトラックで動き回ることで流通過程を一気に短絡化しただけでなく、時間効率も極限まで上げて、迅速な現金化に努めた。実績を積み重ねることで通常の卸業者よりも安く仕入れ、安く卸すことができるようになり、製造者、卸、小売店でWin-Winの関係を築くことができた。当然、その小売店で家具を買い求めるエンドユーザーも、価格面で恩恵を受けたに違いない。

「屋根もないトラックに、背の高いタンスを何本も積んで、傷つけないようにマニラ麻製のロープで縛って固定して……少しでも多く載せるために工夫があったようですね。子どもの眼にも、芸術的な積み方でした」

　父のビジネスは成功し、商圏は九州全域から全国にまで広がった。次第に人が増え、現在の関家具が形作られていく。

One Truck, and His Father

1968 (43th year of Showa Era). Seki's father, current company President Fumihiko Seki, used to drive around in a truck laden with furniture. While Seki's grandfather (Fumihiko's father) was an artisan who made box-shaped items of furniture such as cabinets and chests of drawers his own father trained in the retail trade before going independent as a wholesaler. This was the starting point for SEKI FURNITURE, and remains the foundation of the business today. The sight of his father toiling away is firmly etched into Seki's memories of his childhood.
"In the morning, he would head out in his one truck to stock up at manufacturers. Then he would truck over to the retail stores to turn his stock into cash, which he would then pay to the manufacturers that same evening. He would then repeat this cycle the following day."

In the furniture industry in those days, this was a groundbreaking way of doing business that could even be called revolutionary. It was a given that turning furniture into cash took time due to the complicated distribution channels and the high unit price. It was even common wisdom among the furniture industry in Okawa that payment of accounts was becoming increasingly slack due to the wide spread use of small demonitions and long-term bills. Seki's father punctured a hole into this notion. As well as instantly shortening the distribution process by driving around in his own truck, he also improved time efficiency to the limit, rapidly turning product into cash. Having accrued a track record, he was able to procure more cheaply than other wholesalers, enabling him to wholesale cheaper, creating a winning situation for manufacturers, wholesalers and retailers alike. Naturally, the end users purchasing the furniture from retail stores benefited enormously from the low cost.

"He would stack several tall chests of drawers into this truck which didn't even have a roof, affixing them with a rope made from Manila hemp to stop them getting damaged...he knew exactly how to load in as many as possible. To a child, it looked like a real artistic feat."

工場への憧れ

　現在の関家具とグループ企業のビジネスは、大きくふたつに分けられる。まずは、創業以来の家具の卸業。今では安さだけでなく、良い家具を集めて紹介する、セレクトショップのような立ち位置を大切にしている。家具のプロが、国内だけでなく世界中を回って発見したすばらしい商品を仕入れ、日本でのブランド化までを担う。そしてもうひとつは、卸業としてつかんだニーズを活かし、ゼロから家具の企画を行い、販売までも手がけるファブレスメーカー、いわば家具のSPAとしてのビジネスだ。マーケティングから始まり、デザイン、生産から販売、卸まで一貫して行い、自らブランドを作り、育てている。

　直営店には、現在主に4つの形態がある。古材を用いたビンテージ家具を核とする「クラッシュゲート」、デザイン家具の本場イタリアの手作りソファに特化した「フェデリコセコンド」、快眠をひたすら追求するベッドブランド「シェララフィア」、そして「一枚板」と呼ばれる銘木を素材とした高級家具の専門店「アトリエ木馬」だ。関東・関西の大消費地を中心に、合わせて20店舗以上を展開する。

「私たちには、長年『工場への憧れ』があったんです」

　新卒で父の会社に入社した関には、強い想いがあった。流通に革命を起こした関家具には、風当たりも強かった。結局は中抜きの一形態に過ぎないという批判、やっかみもあった。確かに、ただ利益を乗せて売るだけではつまらない。時代が変わり、流通経路が変わり、必要とされる家具が変わっていく中で、大川では優れた職人や工場が消えていく。培ったネットワークを活かしながら、本当に良いモノを作る人たちと力を合わせ、自分たちのブランドを作っていくことはできないのか。

His father's enterprise was a success, with his business domain broadening out from the whole of Kyushu into the whole country. The number of his staff gradually increased, and the SEKI FURNITURE of today took shape.

A Longing For a Factory

The business of the current SEKI FURNITURE and its group companies can be broadly divided into two strands. First of all, the wholesale business of furniture, which has existed since the company was established. Nowadays, as well as being inexpensive, the company also treasures its position as a "select shop" that collects and introduces outstanding furniture. Furniture professionals go around the country and around the world discovering and procuring top products, aiming to have them penetrate as brands in Japan. Another facet is utilizing needs understood through the wholesale business to design, create and sell furniture from scratch, as a fabless manufacturer in its own right, a business akin to a speciality store retailer for furniture. Through a business model that incorporates the whole process from marketing, design and production, all the way through to sales and wholesale, they create and nurture their very own company brands.

Directly-managed stores ("outlet stores") currently take four main forms:

古材を使った家具を販売する直営店「クラッシュゲート」(東京・自由が丘店)
Outlet store "Crash Gate" (Jiyugaoka Branch) that sells furniture made of used wood.

一枚板の高級家具

　東京・南青山の一角。2013年に「アトリエ木馬」の旗艦店「青山プレミアムギャラリー」がオープンした。ここには、一枚板を天板に使用したダイニングテーブルセットを中心に、数々のアイテムが展示、販売されている。手頃なモノでも20万円前後。中にはカリン、ケヤキや、ローズウッド、さらに入手困難な屋久杉を用いた数百万〜数千万円という商品も並んでいる。これらすべてが、原木の入手から関家具の手によるものだ。

「きっかけは、案外さっぱりしていたのです」

　大川の木工所を辞めて入社してきた社員が、「一枚板の扱いをやりたい」と具申してきた。聞けば、大川市内には仕入れから加工に至るまで高いレベルの業者のネットワークがあるという。そのような高級品が、本当に自分たちのルートで売れるのか。関は半信半疑ながらもその提案を受け入れた。新たに大きな投資が必要になるわけではない。ダメなら止めてしまえばいい。しかし、エンドユーザーの反応は予想外に良かった。

　では、もう少し拡大してみよう。自分たちのアイデアを活かした商品を自ら発注してみよう。せっかくだから、工場を作ろう。それなら、今度はいい材料を直接買い付けてこよう……。こうして、徐々にラインアップは増えていった。

　プロジェクトに携わる社員の中から、一枚板の商品群を直営店でエンドユーザーに直接販売したいという想いを語るものが現れた。そこでまずは他の直営店の一角に置いてみたが、スペースが限られ反応は今ひとつだった。そんなはずはない、一か八かの勝負をする価値はきっとある。新宿に思い切って一枚板専門の直営店を出したところ、それまでが嘘のように良い売れ行きを示したという。

「かつては、一枚板の商品群は、発想さえなかった。必要とされる家具、魅

"Crash Gate" of which the core product is vintage furniture made from used materials; the "Federico II Italia" series, which specializes in hand-made sofas rooted in genuine Italian design; the "Schlaraffia" bed brand, which provides a pleasant sleep, and the "ATELIER MOKUBA" series, which is a specialist high-grade furniture store that uses single planks of rare and precious wood as its raw material. There are more than 20 stores altogether, centered on the major markets consuming regions of Kanto and Kansai.

"For a long time, we had a certain longing for a factory."

Seki, who entered his father's company upon graduating, had a strong resolve. SEKI FURNITURE, while revolutionizing distribution, was also the subject of envy and criticism: that their business was ultimately just another form of cutting out the middleman. Indeed, there was nothing interesting about simply tacking on a profit and selling. As the era changed, so did distribution channels; and amid changes to the kind of furniture needed, preeminent craftsmen and factories began to disappear from Okawa. Could Seki draw on his network and pool resources with people who shared the desire to make top quality products, and create their own brand?

Opulent Furniture From One Single Sheet of Timber

A corner of Minami Aoyama, Tokyo. "AOYAMA PREMIUM GALLERY," the flagship store of "ATELIER MOKUBA," opened in 2013. This store displays and sells numerous items, centered on dining table sets that use one single sheet of wood for the tabletop. Even the moderately-priced items still sell for around 200,000 yen. There are also creations ranging from millions of yen to tens of millions of yen - using Burmese rosewood, Japanese zelkova, rosewood and even Yakushima cedar which is extremely difficult to obtain. SEKI FURNITURE created all of these, down to the procurement of raw wood.

"The starting point was less complicated than you might think."

A new employee who had resigned from a post at a woodworking plant in

力的と思われる家具が変わってきていることを、改めて強く感じました」

4000万円のテーブルはなぜ売れるのか？

　畳の上に置かれたちゃぶ台を囲む一家団らんは、もはや映画やドラマの中の遠い「昭和」の風景になりつつある。住宅やマンションでリビング・ダイニングが当たり前になり、ダイニングテーブルと椅子のセット、そしてソファとテーブルの組み合わせが、どんな家庭でもありふれた風景になった。

「私たち家具の業界人にとって、もともと一枚板とは、まさに和室で使う座卓の高級品として提案してきたもので、和室がなくなった以上、一枚板の魅力も忘れ去られていたのです」

　ダイニングテーブルにはもっぱら南洋材が用いられるし、安くて加工のしやすい合板が重宝された。一枚板の魅力である自然な風合いは、むしろ加工の過程で切り落とされる運命でさえあった。しかし、関家具の挑戦は、あえて一枚板の耳（皮）を残し、人工的な加工をなるべく加えない形でありながら、現代の住宅に合う実用的なダイニングテーブルセットを作ることだった。決して安くな

一枚板を専門に取り扱う直営店「アトリエ木馬」の旗艦店「青山プレミアムギャラリー」
"AOYAMA PREMIUM GALLERY," the flagship store of "ATELIER MOKUBA," the outlet store specializing in goods fashioned from one sheet of wood.

Okawa came to Seki, stating that he wanted to deal in products made from a single sheet of wood. Apparently, there was a network in Okawa City of highly skilled merchants, spanning procurement all the way to processing. If Seki and his team could make such opulent goods, would Seki Furniture be able to sell them through their distribution routes? While dubious about the viability of this venture, Seki accepted the proposal. It wasn't as though new major investment was required. If it flopped then he could just give up on the venture. However, the reaction from customers was much better than expected.

So, maybe we will try expanding this a little more. While we are at it, why not commission products using our own original ideas. In fact, we might as well build a factory. In which case, we should go and directly purchase good materials ourselves. In this way, the line-up steadily increased.

Among employees involved in the project, there were those who expressed a desire to directly sell the product range using a single sheet of wood to end-users at outlet stores. They decided to place the products in a corner of another outlet store, but the space was limited and the reaction was less than optimum. This surely could not be the case; it was worth throwing caution to the wind and playing a high-stakes game. When they took the gamble of opening an outlet store in Shinjuku, products sold so well that it was hard to believe the series of events leading up to that point.

"There was a time where I never even had the notion of a group of products fashioned from one sheet of wood. I felt anew that the kind of furniture people wanted, the kind of furniture that appealed to people – was changing."

What Explains the Sales of Tables Costing 40 Million Yen?

The days of a family gathered around a table atop a tatami floor have become something you only see in films or dramas about the old times. Modern houses and apartments have a living and dining room as standard; a dining table and chairs in a set, and a sofa and table set has become a common feature of any household.

いにもかかわらず、これがユーザーに受け入れられたのだ。もっとも高級なものでは、4000万円以上する一枚板のテーブルを売った実績がある。

　しかも、一枚板は100年でも200年でも伝えていくことができる。表面を0.2ミリ削るだけで天然の美しい「木肌」が現れ、新品同様になる。持っているだけで今後も価格は上がるだろうから、本心では売りたくなかった面もあるという。

　関家具のスタッフは、やがて木材の良し悪しを見抜く力や情報力もついていった。中身の見えない丸太には、独特の鑑識眼が要求される。世界中のマーケットにネットワークを張り、良いモノがあればすぐ飛んでいく。

「今、世界中で高級木材の価格が上昇している。ニーズは増している一方、自然は保護しなければなりませんから。将来を見据えて、今はストックも手がけているところです」

自由な社風の経営者がかける言葉

　何代にもわたって使い続けられる一枚板のテーブル。それを目の当たりにした時の神秘的な風合い、そして得られる心の豊かさは金銭価値には代えがたいものがある。私は、同時になぜ関家具がそうしたチャレンジをすることができたのかにも、強く関心を抱く。入ったばかりの社員、若い社員が提案し、それがどんどん採用され、ブラッシュアップされ、その上ビジネスとしてしっかりと成功を収めているのだから。相当に優秀なスタッフを継続してスカウトできているのか、それとも教育研修の制度が優れているのか。あるいは、場の作り方、ファシリテーションが巧みなのか。

　2015年は30人以上を新規採用したという。私はそこに、ブランディングが生み出す成果の一端を感じる。彼らが関家具にやってきてくれた理由は、何な

"For us insiders in the furniture industry, one sheet of wood would only ever be used for an opulent low table to adorn a Japanese-style room; as these rooms became a thing of the past, so too did the appeal of a single sheet of wood."

Dining tables these days use entirely tropical woods, and in particular plywood which is cheap and easy to process. The natural texture of one sheet of wood, which is its main appeal, could have ended up being trimmed off in the processing stage. However, the challenge for SEKI FURNITURE was to retain the skin of the plank of wood and to avoid as much as possible man-made processing, while still creating a practical dining table that fits the modern household. While definitely not cheap, they were well received by consumers. The most opulent products included a table fashioned from one single plank of timber that sold for more than 40 million yen.

What is more, a single sheet of timber will last 100 or even 200 years down the line. Simply trimming 0.2mm off the surface reveals naturally beautiful "tree skin," which looks as good as new. The value of such wood will only increase over time, a fact that made Seki somewhat reluctant to sell it.

Over time, staff at SEKI FURNITURE developed the ability to discern between good and poor quality wood, as well as accruing a great deal of knowledge. A unique discerning eye is required for a log of which the inside cannot be seen. Casting a network over markets around the world, they would swiftly head over to wherever high quality wood appeared.

"Presently, the value of high-quality wood is rising around the world. While needs are increasing, on the other hand we must protect nature. In anticipation of such a future, we are in the process of stocking up."

Words From a Manager Who Favors a Free Working Atmosphere

A table fashioned from a single plane of wood, which can be passed down the generations. The almost mysterious texture that one experiences when encountering it for the first time, and the way it enriches your very being is

のだろうか。

「当社の社風は、とにかく自由にやってもらうこと。社長をはじめ、各自がやりたいことをやる会社で、正直に言うとブランド作りも含め、あまり計画性があったわけではないのです」

関のこの言葉は、半分は謙遜にせよ、もう半分は本音なのかもしれない。ただ私には、関の口からいくつかのヒントとなるキーワードが聞き取れた。

「あっ、それ、面白そうじゃん!」

「ダメならやめればいい、それは仕方ない」

「失敗したことは責めない」

「褒めて伸ばします」

新入社員は九州だけでなく、今や全国から集まる。福岡ヤフオク!ドームの広告を増やしたこともあり、最近は九州の全企業で就職したい企業ランキング30位台に入ったという。

「びっくりしています。しかも、家具がやりたい、という純粋な人ばかり入ってきてくれるのが嬉しいですよね」

青山プレミアムギャラリーには、常時100枚以上の無垢一枚板が展示されている
In the AOYAMA PREMIUM GALLERY, more than 100 sheets of pure one-sheet timber are on display permanently.

something that cannot be given a price tag. At the same time, I am personally very interested in why SEKI FURNITURE was able to rise to this challenge. A new and young employee proposed the idea, which was adopted over and over, then perfected and is now doing very well as a business. Is it down to the ability to continually scout excellent employees, or is it down to an excellent training system? Or, is it down to being able to deftly create and facilitate a certain culture?

In 2015, the new intake of employees was more than 30 people. In this fact, I get a sense of the fruits created by branding. What was it that attracted them to SEKI FURNITURE?

"The company atmosphere is basically pretty free. It is a company where the president and each employee can do what they want, and to be honest, even when it comes to brand building, nothing is planned to any degree."

Seki's words might be half modesty and half his real sentiment. I did, however, pick up on various keywords that came out from Seki's mouth:
"Yes, that looks very interesting!"
"If it is not going to work out then give up on it, nothing you can do."
"I don't blame people for failing."
"People who are praised will grow."

New employees are not just from Kyushu, but come from all over the country. SEKI FURNITURE also increased advertising in FUKUOKA YAFUOKU! DOME which might explain why the it managed to enter the list of top 30 companies in Kyushu that graduates want to work for among all companies in Kyushu.
"I can't believe it. Most of all, I am so happy that they are all people purely passionate about creating furniture."

Talented Employees Seek Out Companies With Clear and Defined Branding That Resounds With Them

Take one employee who entered the company this year. This episode would

ブランディングが明確な企業には、共鳴する社員が集まる

　今年入社した、ある社員。そのエピソードは、現在の関家具の活力を象徴しているかのようだった。

　ある日、新宿の「アトリエ木馬」の直営店から、関あてに電話が入る。高校生が来て、将来関家具に入社してこうした製品を手がけるにはどんな大学に進学したらいいのか、と聞かれたという。あるテレビドラマの撮影に、関家具は協力した。そこで使われた一枚板の家具を見て関家具を知り、新宿の店を探し当てて直接話を聞こうと思ったという。その想いは真剣そのものだった。関は直感した。「大学に行かなくていい。すぐ採用する」

　こうして、この春から関家具の一員になったという。関家具の生み出す商品、それらが織り成すブランドに惚れ込む。そして自ら足を運び、積極的に道を切り拓こうとするフットワーク。私はこの話に、ブランドが果たす仲間集めの好例を見る。ブランディングが明確な企業には、共鳴する社員が集まってくるのだ。

「社長も私も、いいアイデアはないのか、企画書を出せと要求したことはありません。それでも、どんどん面白い企画が出てくる」

　年齢もあまり関係はない。「アトリエ木馬」を実質的に取り仕切っている責任者は30代前半。それで工場の60人を束ねている。女性社員たちも自らのモノの見方を活かした提案を出してくる。関家具で扱っている家具、作っている家具は良いモノだが、同時にそこに携わっている人たちに、揺るぎない自信がある。4000万円のテーブルがなぜ4000万円なのか、いくらでも丁寧に、詳細に自分の言葉で説明できる。言われてしているのではない。自ら、それも心から思って取り組む仕事。そこには顧客の心を打つブランドが宿るのだ。

seem to symbolize the current vitality of SEKI FURNITURE.

One day, Seki received a direct phone call form an "ATELIER MOKUBA" outlet in Shinjuku. A high school student had turned up, explaining that he wanted to work for SEKI FURNITURE and create a certain kind of furniture in future; and in order to do so, which university should he attend? SEKI FURNITURE had been featured in a drama on television. This had led to the high school student learning about SEKI FURNITURE's creations from one single plank of wood, and had proceeded to look up the store in Shinjuku and go there in person.

This teenager was absolutely serious. Seki could sense it. "You don't need to go to university. Come and work for me."

Thus, he/she became a SEKI FURNITURE employee from this spring, having fallen in love with the products created by SEKI FURNITURE and the brands it interweaves. This had prompted him/her to go there in person and to cultivate a path. I see this as a good example of how a brand can pull like-minded people together. Companies that are explicitly and determinably branded will bring in people who thoroughly endorse the message that the company emits. "The president and I make a point of never ordering employees to come up with new ideas or produce detailed plans. Despite this, all these interesting projects materialize."

Age is not an issue. The person in charge of actually running "ATELIER MOKUBA" is in his/her early 30s, bringing together all 60 people in the factory. Female employees are empowered to inject their creativity in a way they see fit. Whilst the items stocked and fashioned at SEKI FURNITURE are excellent, there is also a notable unswerving confidence in the people who work there. They can eloquently explain in their own words the reasons why a 40 million yen table costs 40 million yen. They are not parroting something they were instructed to say. Each employee puts heart and soul into their work. Within this lies the brand that strikes a chord with customers.

サインを汲み取れ

「社員はもっとも有能な社長の先生である」。これは、父・関文彦社長が大切にしている心得のひとつである。ただ、社員はあくまでスタッフであり、先生ではない。つまり、社員を有能な先生にするには、何らかの工夫が必要になるはずだ。一枚板の「アトリエ木馬」だけではない。ビンテージテイストの「クラッシュゲート」も、従来の関家具の発想では古材を家具に加工しようというアイデアは出なかっただろうと関は振り返る。

「低価格帯の商品開発を期待して採用した中途社員が、自ら出してきたアイデアだったんです。最初はビンテージがこんなに受け入れられ、売れるなんて思ってもいませんでした」

しかし、社員たちに「そう言わせた」のは間違いなく関家具という会社である。アイデアがあふれ出る現場とは、どういうものなのだろうか。

実際は関家具も企業だ。経営者と従業員、上司と部下、先輩と後輩、社歴の長短、部署や担当の違いなど、いくらでも立場の違いがあるし、遠慮が生まれてしまう。

「私の経験上、関家具に集まってくれた人は必ず何かしら関家具でやりたいことを持っていて、ときどき、リラックスしている場面でふとそのサイン、信号を出す。私の仕事は、その微妙なサインを逃さず、汲み上げることなんです」

ちょっと待って、今の話、詳しく聞かせてよ!

そして、先ほど述べたような言葉をかけ、どんどんアイデアを引き出していく。それが現実化し、実績を挙げれば評価される。失敗しても、GOサインを出したのは経営側だから責められない。

「大人数の会議なんて意見も出ないし、得てして主宰者の独演会で終わる。

Picking up on signs

"Employees are a CEO's most capable teachers." This was one maxim favored by Seki's father, Fumihiko.

At the end of the day, employees are staff, not teachers. Put simply, to turn employees into capable teachers requires a certain amount of ingenuity. The "ATELIER MOKUBA" series fashioned from one sheet of wood is not the only example. Seki ruminates that the vintage "Crash Gate" furniture – made from used materials – also would not have emanated from the original Seki line of thought.

"This was an idea that came from a mid-career employee who we had taken on hoping he would develop products in the low price range. To begin with, we had no idea that vintage would be so popular and would sell so well."

However, if there is any company that encourages its employees to "let it out," it is SEKI FURNITURE. How do you create a company where ideas spring forth so plentifully?

When all is said and done, SEKI FURNITURE is a company. There are managers and employees, people pulling rank, people who have been there longer than newcomers, various managerial politics and so on, all of which makes people become standoffish in sharing their ideas.

"In my experience, people who come to work at SEKI FURNITURE will usually have something in mind that they want to do, and sometimes when you are in an informal setting it is my job to pick up on those covert signs, the hidden signals. I tell them to slow down, track back and tell me the whole picture!"

Then, he addresses employees using the exhortations mentioned above, drawing ideas out of them one by one. These take shape, and if successful, will be acknowledged. If it goes wrong, it was the top brass that gave the go sign so there is no scapegoating.

"No-one gets to voice their opinions in big meetings, which can end up being a one-way solo recital by the president. You might as well just make a series of

だったら告知すればすむことですよ」

フラットな場でリラックスさせ、微妙なヒントを拾う。それが、一層ブランドの価値を強めていく秘密なのだ。

ブランドで集まった人材は、ブランドを誇り、高めていく

私が関家具の最大の強みと考えるのは、ブランディングこそがブランドの強さを高め、企業を成長させるという仕組みが極めてうまく機能している点だ。ブランドに惹かれて集まった人材は、ブランドを誇り、より良い仕事をし、結果ブランド価値をさらに高めていく。そして、さらに優秀な人材が集まっていく。しかも、関の言葉を信じるのであれば、それがナチュラルに達成されているというのだから、関家具の企業文化は驚愕に値する。

今後、関家具がさらに成長することは間違いないだろうが、社員数が増え、あるいは上場を果たした後、このすばらしい企業文化をどう継承し、発展させていくかが重要なテーマになる。すべての社員、すべての仲間からアイデアを汲み取り続けることがもし可能なら、それはとても幸福な企業の姿だ。しかし良いブランドを構築した企業は必ず成長する。いや、成長しないはずがない。その時、たったひとりの経営者が汲み上げられるサインは、必ず限界が来てしまうことは、想定しなければならないだろう。

物理的な限界をどう乗り越え、すばらしい企業文化を継承し、発展させていくのか。それが、これからの関家具の新しいチャレンジになるのだろう。

「私自身、同族経営、家族経営ということについては、肯定的な考えも否定的な考えも持っていません。ただ、私がひとりでやれることなんて、現時点でとうに限界を超えています。だからこそ、将来的には会社をよりパブリックにしてい

announcements."

Enable employees to relax in a convivial setting, and pick up on signs they give off. At one level, this is the secret to bolstering brand value.

A Workforce That Resonates With a Brand Will Take Pride in it, and Take it to a Higher Level

In my view, the major strength of SEKI FURNITURE lies in the fact that it is thoroughly underpinned by a highly functioning system through which the branding reinforces itself. Employees, who seek out the brand end up becoming proud of it, and work in a better way, and as a result end up elevating the brand. This has the effect of bringing in even more talented employees. And, if you take Seki at his word, that this is all achieved organically, it translates to a truly astonishing corporate culture.

Suffice to say that while SEKI FURNITURE will continue to grow, at some point the question will arise of how it will be possible to transmit this amazing corporate culture forward once the number of employees grows and the company goes public. A company is certainly very lucky if it is truly able to continually pick up on all the hints and ideas from its employees and partners. The fact remains, however, that if you build a strong brand then the company will grow. It simply cannot fail to grow. At such a point, one must envisage that there inevitably comes a limit to the hints and clues that one single manager is able to pick up on.

How should one overcome the physical limits to being able to pass on an amazing company culture and develop it further? This will surely become a challenge to be handled by SEKI FURNITURE in the coming years.
"With regard to myself and running this as a family business, I have neither positive nor negative feelings. That said, at the present moment I am already going beyond what I can handle by myself. For this very reason, we have to think about the company becoming more public from now on."

くことを考えなければいけないと思います」

フラットな場、自由な雰囲気を保ちながら、同じ志を持つ仲間なら誰でも持続していける制度を構築する試み。関家具になら、きっとできるはずだ。

海外へ広がる夢

関家具がブランドを自ら打ち出したことで、拓けてきた可能性がある。それは、ジャパン・ブランドの一翼を担う海外進出だ。木材価格の上昇は、木材を使った家具の世界的な人気の高まりを示しているという。

「引き合いはすでに各方面から来ています。すでに輸出は始めていますし、直営店をドバイに出店しないか、などという誘いも舞い込み始めています」

関家具は、決して日本産の木材にこだわっているわけではない。東南アジア、アフリカ、北米などから良い木材を買い付けてくるし、世界のすばらしい家具を発掘するバイヤーでもあるのだが、そこで知り合った現地の木材や家具のプロたちは、口を揃えて関家具を評価してくれるのだという。特に、中国での評価は高いそうだ。

「私たちの作るような家具は、現地にはあまりないそうなんです」

英語版のホームページを開けば世界から注文が舞い込む。新宿や青山の「アトリエ木馬」には、外国人客の姿が目に見えて増えてきた。

「『アトリエ木馬』の店をニューヨークに出したい、と社員たちが言い始めています。いきなりど真ん中に出て行って、そこから周辺に広げていこうという意気込みなんです。初めて新宿に直営店を出した時に比べれば、みんな確信を持ってやっていますよ」

自動車やエレクトロニクスだけではない、メイド・イン・ジャパンのブランド化を、

Endeavoring to create a system conducive to a flat workplace, which has a free atmosphere where like-minded people can work together, on a sustainable basis. If anybody can do it, it is SEKI FURNITURE.

Dreams That Fan Out Overseas

There are possibilities that have opened up through SEKI FURNITURE spelling out its brand. This is the planning of a role in the overseas advance of the Japan Brand. The rising price for wood materials strongly suggests that the popularity of wooden furniture is rising around the world.

"Business inquiries are coming from all quarters. We are starting to export and offers are starting to flow in from overseas, including regarding an outlet store in Dubai."

SEKI FURNITURE does not insist that all wood has to come from Japan, going abroad to purloin high quality wood from Southeast Asia, South Africa and North America. While managing to be a buyer that discovers amazing furniture from afar, SEKI FURNITURE is held in high regard by the wood and furniture professions that it encounters on its travels to uncover the very best wood. A particularly high reputation is enjoyed in China.

"Apparently, you cannot get hold of the kind of furniture that we make locally."

Launching an English website led to a flood of orders. The "ATELIER MOKUBA" stores in Shinjuku and Aoyama were visibly inundated with foreign customers.

"Employees have started to say that they want to open a "ATELIER MOKUBA" store in New York. They are excited to throw themselves into the fray, and then expand from there. Compared to when we opened a store in Shinjuku, they are all pretty confident about what they are doing."

When it comes promulgating the "Made in Japan brand," manufacturers such as Seki feel that they are on the global frontline, right up there with automobile and electronics manufacturers. When it comes to advancing overseas, SEKI FURNITURE is keen to map out a course as a brand that is

関たちも世界の最前線で感じている。単に、国内の需要が頭打ちだから、というだけではない。海外に出て行く以上は、もっとも自信のある自分たちのブランド、それも最高級品を、日本というブランドで打ち出していきたいと語る。

「日本国のおかげ、というのは最近痛感するばかりです。まず最初に、日本の会社だから信用してもらえる。先輩諸氏に感謝しながら、そこを最大限活用させてもらい、頑張っていきたい」

ふるさと大川の復活

世界への夢と同時に、関にはもうひとつの強い思いがある。それは、大川の復活だ。

「全国のエンドユーザー、家具ファンが大川に来てくれるような、そして家具作りを志す人が集えるような街にしたい」

関家具は1975（昭和50）年、大川に「びっくり市（現関家具本店）」を開設した。計9棟にわたる広い店内に、国内外各メーカーと自社ブランドを揃えている。室町時代以来、500年近い家具の生産地として栄えてきた大川だが、意外にもエンドユーザーが回遊できる場所は少ない。それを何とかしようという試みの一貫だ。

「年に2回『木工祭（大川木工まつり）』というイベントがある日を除けば、大川に来てくれるエンドユーザーは多くありません。あくまで製造業者と卸業者の街ですから、小売は弱い」

しかも、数々の匠の技が消えつつある。

「部品、ネジ、削り、塗装、組み立て専門の伝統技術『組子』……細かい分野ごとに得意な技を持っている企業は、今でも500社はあるはずです」

confident in itself, a brand that offers Japanese products that are of unrivaled opulence.

"Recently, I cannot but help feel how grateful I am to Japan. First and foremost, we want to inspire trust as a Japanese company. Remaining thankful to the original pioneers our we want to stand on their shoulders and keep the fire burning bright."

Revitalizing Okawa, a Place That Means Home

As well as dreams of global expansion, Seki is committed to revitalizing Okawa.

"We want to create a town that brings together potential customers from around Japan with furniture fans and other people interested in creating furniture."

SEKI FURNITURE established "Bikkuri Ichi" (currently the main SEKI FURNITURE store) in Okawa in 1975 (Showa 50). Spanning nine buildings, the cavernous store has a large selection of items from Japanese and overseas manufactures as well as own-company brands. Since the Muromachi Era (1336-1573), for nearly 500 years, Okawa has flourished as a furniture producing area; however, there are not many places where potential customers can migrate to. This is one of many attempts to address the issue.

"Apart from the two days a year when the "Woodwork Festival" (Okawa Woodwork Festival) is held, no customers come all the way to Okawa. Due to it being essentially a realm of manufacturers and wholesalers, retail is not so strong."

Unfortunately, many artisan techniques are fading away.

"I would say there are about 500 companies remaining who still have the inch-perfect expertise, the traditional techniques for parts, screws, wood shaving, coating, assemblage and so on."

Behind the quality of these dining tables, fashioned from one single plank of

一枚板のダイニングテーブルのクオリティを可能にしたのは、こうした圧倒的な産業としてのバックグラウンドの厚みだった。それが今、危機に瀕している。職人が消えれば、家具は作れない。市内の生産高は、ピーク時の5分の1以下だ。すでに、大川以外の日本の家具産地も大きく衰退しつつある。

　大川から始まった関家具だからこそ、できること、しなければならないことがある。自社の直営店を通じた販売の強化。世界に通じる技術を持った工場の育成、買収。課題は多い。

「いずれは大川に家具の学校を作りたいですね。地域の皆さんと一緒に考えていきたい。ここは私のふるさとでもありますから」

　良いブランドがあれば、売れる。ならば同時に、志のある人をこの世界に残すことも、大切なミッションだと感じている。

家具以外と勝負するブランディング

　JR九州の九州新幹線や、豪華寝台列車「ななつ星」の木のぬくもりを活かした日本的な内装は、実は大川の職人たちの手による仕事だ。そして、これまで家具に関心のなかった人たちからも好評を得ているという。数十万円、数百万円、あるいはそれ以上の高級一枚板テーブルを売ってきた関には、ひとつ見えてきたものがある。

「果たして数千万円のテーブルを売る時、私たちは本当に家具屋として勝負しているのだろうか？」

　これまでは、どうすればいい家具を安く売れるか、ライバルよりも売上を伸ばせるか、家具業界でシェアを伸ばせるかを考えてきた。それ自体は、家具の世界に限らず、どんな企業、どの業界でも変わらない意識だろう。しかし、数

wood, is such a strong background rooted in industry. This industry is currently in crisis. If the artisans disappear, furniture will not get made. The production output within the city is one-fifth of what it was at its peak. And already, other furniture manufacturing areas in Japan apart from Okawa are in the grip of demise.

SEKI FURNITURE traces its roots to Okawa and by token, has various things to offer as well as obligations to fulfill. Strengthening sales through directly owned outlets. Growing and acquiring factories with technology that connects with the world. There are many challenges.

"Eventually, I would like to establish a furniture school in Okawa. I would like to involve everybody in the community to think about how to do it – please remember, this is my home town."

A good brand sells. Given this, I also feel that it is an important mission to ensure that people who share the same desire remain in the (furniture) world.

Branding That Can Compete Outside of Furniture

The JR Kyushu Bullet Train and the "Seven Stars" luxury sleeper trains both have Japanese-inspired interiors that give off the warmth of wood; these interiors are actually the work of artisans from Okawa. Apparently, they have also provoked a positive reaction in people who have never been interested in furniture before. For Seki, who has sold opulent tables fashioned from one plane of wood for several hundred thousand yen and even several million yen, something became apparent.

"If we actually sell a table for tens of million yen, are we really being competitive as a furniture store?"

Until now, the preoccupations were how cheap you could sell furniture, to what degree you could out-perform your rivals, how big you could grow your share of the furniture market. This fact itself is not limited to the furniture industry and is presumably a prevalent idea in companies in all sectors. However, people who are willing to spend several million yen on a table

百万円のテーブルを買う人は、よその店舗より一割安かったから関家具を選んでくれたわけでは恐らくないはずだ。超富裕層ならまだしも、きっとクルマを買い換えようか、ファーストクラスに乗ってバカンスに出かけようか、あるいは一幅の絵や書画を求めようか、といった選択肢と比較した上で、関家具のテーブルを選んでくれたはずなのだ。

　家具の需要は今後も大きくは回復しないだろう。結婚する女性に婚礼ダンスを持たせることも、引っ越しと同時に洋服ダンスや食器棚を揃える機会も減ってしまった。それはハウジングメーカーやマンションディベロッパーがクローゼットや物入れとして提案するものに変わり、家具職人の出る幕ではなくなってしまったからだ。かつて、大川の家具職人のエースは、婚礼家具を手がける人だったという。そこには、強いプライドがあった。

「関家具がブランドを作る意味は、もしかしたら家具であって家具でない世界に漕ぎ出すタイミングだからなのかもしれません」

　関家具のブランディングは、大川を、そして日本の家具作りを変えていく。そんな想いを、関は静かに語っているようだった。

株式会社関家具
所在地　〒831-0033　福岡県大川市幡保201-1
創業　昭和43年（1968年）4月
設立　昭和57年（1982年）11月2日
資本金　1億4000万円
代表者　代表取締役　関　文彦
事業内容　家具・インテリア・住関連商品企画販売

probably do not choose SEKI FURNITURE because it is ten percent cheaper than other stores. Unless they are a member of the ultra-wealthy strata, people choose a table fashioned by SEKI FURNITURE after comparing this purchase with other options such as whether to purchase a new car, or whether to travel first class on a luxury holiday abroad, or whether to buy a piece of fine art.

 The demand for furniture will is not likely to recover significantly in the coming years. It is less and less a custom to give a chest of drawers as a wedding present, and when people move into new houses, they no longer need clothes dressers and food cupboards. This is because housing manufacturers and apartment developers now offer a solution with built-in closets and cupboards, relegating the furniture craftsmen to the sidelines. There was a time when the elite artisans at Okawa Furniture were those who crafted marital-related furniture. Within this, a strong brand existed.
"The significance of SEKI FURNITURE creating a brand could in fact lie in this being an opportune moment to set out into another realm that may or may not be furniture-related."

 SEKI FURNITURE's branding could be a force for change in Okawa, and indeed in furniture creation in Japan. This was a notion that Seki articulated to me.

Company Profile:
SEKI FURNITUE Co., Ltd.
Address: 201-1 Hataho, Okawa-shi, Fukuoka 831-0033
Established: November 2, 1982
Capital: JPY 140 million
Representative: Fumihiko Seki, President
Business Description: Planning and sales of furniture and home interior products.

未来に続く

企業ブランディングが切り開く、ジャパン・ブランドの未来

イマジナ　代表取締役社長
関野吉記（よしき）

イマジナの企業ブランディングは、
なぜ世界とつながっているのか？
海外で成功する企業は、何が違うのか？

イマジナの事業は企業ブランディング。
企業理念をカルチャーブックにまとめ、
理念に根ざした人事制度をオーダーメイドで構築し、
運用・浸透までトータルに提供している。
ブランディングが顧客だけでなく、
社員や株主などステークホルダーを集め、増やす。
日本で、世界で、企業を成長させる、そのブランディングの仕組みとは？

文中、敬称略

To Be Continued

CORPORATE BRANDING TO CUT A PATH FOR THE FUTURE OF JAPAN BRANDS

President and CEO, imajina,inc.
Yoshiki Sekino

Why is imajina's corporate branding connected to the world? What is different about companies that succeed abroad?

imajina is in the business of corporate branding.
Compiling company philosophies into culture books, imajina constructs order-made personnel systems rooted in these principles, providing total support, encompassing operation and permeation.
As well as customers, branding attracts and increases the number of overall stakeholders, including employees and shareholders.
What is the system behind such branding that drives the growth of companies in Japan and around the world?

ブランディングは
何のためにある？

　私たちイマジナを一言で説明するなら、「企業ブランディングを手がけている企業」ということになる。イマジナは、主に5つのサービスを通して、企業や地域、市町村、公共団体などのブランディングを支援している。

　まず、「カルチャーブック」の作成。時間をかけたインタビューをもとに、クライアントのビジョン、ミッション、バリューの3つの視点からフィロソフィーを創出。従業員一人ひとりの成長を促すため、スタンスやマニュアルとして業務に落とし込むための冊子としてまとめ、組織活性化や人材活用に役立ててもらう。ただ文章が羅列されているのではなく、わかりやすい言葉やイメージキャラクターなどのイラストを使いながら、より多くの人に企業の想いを理解してもらうよう表現する。

　たとえば、ある企業からは、創業30周年の節目として、改めて創業者の想いをまとめ、今後のビジョンを明確にし、社員に自社を誇りに思ってもらいたいという願いから、カルチャーブックの制作依頼をいただいた。制作当初は、何か特別なことをしたわけでもなく、他社と同じようなことを言っているだけなので、不安だったという。ところが、カルチャーブックができあがってからは、今までうまく言葉で表現できなかったことが、ストーリーとしてうまく整理されたことで、社員それぞれの意識に自社のカルチャーが根付き始めているそうだ。今では、全社員がカルチャーブックを持ち歩くほど好評をいただいている。

　ただし、カルチャーブックは、カルチャー浸透の起点であり、その後に浸透に向けた取り組みを行わなければ、カルチャーの浸透・定着は難しい。そこで、「人事制度」や「研修」を、創出したフィロソフィーに基づいて構築する。さらに、グローバルでの企業成長を支援する「アメリカ進出サポート」や、人材の見える化を実現するクラウド型人事評価システム「jiina」も提供している。

　2006年に設立したイマジナは、一貫してブランディングの大切さを訴えてきた。そこには、海外に進出する日本企業を1500社以上サポートしてきた私たちの眼から見て、日本の企業が持っているポテンシャルを最大化したい、という想いがある。日本の企業が持っているすばらしい理念、優秀な経営者たちの考えを、まとまりあるメッセージとして世界に明確に発信できれば、企業価値を高め、結果としてステークホルダーを増やせるのではないか、という想いがある。

　本書では、私が考える企業ブランディングとはいったい何なのか、そしてどのように

What is the Point of Branding?

If I were to sum up imajina in one phrase, it would be "a corporation involved in corporate branding." Through five main services, imajina supports branding for companies and communities, municipalities, and public bodies.

Firstly, creating "culture books." Based on lengthy interviews, imajina construct a philosophy from the three perspectives of vision, mission and value. To encourage the growth of each individual employee, imajina compiles a booklet embodying these elements into a stance and a manual, in order for them to be applied to work. This in turn helps to revitalize the organization and utilize personnel effectively. Rather than merely using lengthy blocks of text, imajina uses clear language and image characters, as well as illustrations, to make a company's philosophy as accessible as possible.

Consider this example: A corporation that had reached the 30-year mark in its history approached imajina to create a culture book with the intention of freshly summarizing the philosophy of the founder, clarifying its future vision, and enabling employees to feel proud of their company. To begin with, this company was anxious, feeling that imajina had not done anything particularly special and that they were merely saying the same things as other companies. Yet once the culture book was complete, ideas that the management had been unable to articulate up until then were succinctly woven into a story, allowing the culture of the company to take root in each of the employee's minds. Apparently, this culture book is so popular that all employees carry it around with them.

However, culture books only provide the starting point for culture to permeate; unless they are followed up with initiatives toward its osmosis, it will be hard for the culture to actually take hold. Thus, imajina construct a human resource system and training course based on the newly created philosophy. It also provides "support for advancing into America" to propel global corporate growth, and the Internet-based performance management system "jiina" to render human resources more visible.

Founded in 2006, imajina has consistently emphasized the importance of branding. Having supported more than 1,500 Japanese companies make an overseas foray, imajina has the desire to fully maximize the potential inherent in Japanese companies. This is the desire that if the excellent principles of Japanese companies and the excellent ideas of their managers can be encapsulated into a message and clearly communicated to the world, it will be possible to enhance corporate value, and as a result, increase stakeholders.

In this book, while introducing real examples of various companies, I have looked into what I consider corporate branding to actually mean, and how

ブランディングをするのかについて、さまざまな企業のケースを具体的にご紹介しながら考えてきた。その締めくくりとして、この章では、私たちイマジナの考えを述べながら、同時に「企業ブランディングは、何のためにするのか」という根本的な問いについて、私なりの答えを述べていきたい。

ブランディングは
成長を左右する

もし、あなたが発注の権限を握っているとして、価格もクオリティもほぼ同等な企業が2社並んでいたら、何を基準に選ぶだろうか。もし、自分の息子や娘が、ネームバリューも報酬もほぼ同等なふたつの企業から内定を得たら、どちらに就職させたいだろうか。恐らく、ほとんどの人が、より「いい会社」を選択するのではないかと思う。

企業理念がすばらしいこと。社員を大切にし、社会に貢献していること。目指しているゴールが明確であること。そして、それらが作り出す企業としてのブランドが明確であること。もしかすると、多少価格が高くても、あるいは多少ネームバリューや報酬が低くても、より優れたブランドを持っている企業を選ぶケースだってあるかもしれない。

ステークホルダーを増やしたければ、良い人材を確保したければ、ブランディングは不可欠になる。どんな歴史ある大企業でも、ブランドが崩壊すれば、あっという間にステークホルダーの心は離れていってしまう。ベンチャーや中小企業には、なかなか良い人材が来てくれないという声が多い。人口の変化、少子高齢化の影響や景気の回復もあって、今や優秀な人材は取り合いになっている。一方、まるで進学先を偏差値で選ぶかのような、ネームバリュー重視、報酬と安定性優先の企業選びが、日本経済の活力を奪ってきたことも次第に認識されつつある。早くから自分の得意な分野を伸ばし、専門性を高められる企業に就職することも、今では決してない話ではない。やりたいことがいきなり、しかも若いうちから思いきりできることは、何にも代えがたい魅力なのだ。

ただ、その際にブランドがなければ、いったいどうやって就職希望者に自社の魅力を訴えることができるだろうか。ステークホルダーとつながり、優秀な人材を確保するために、ブランディングは必須である。それは、企業の成長を左右する。

クオリティだけでなく、
想いを輸出する

ところで、ご覧いただいた通り、本書は

it is implemented. To round off, in this chapter, while presenting the ideas held by us at imajina, I would like to offer some of my own responses to the quintessential question of "what exactly is corporate branding for?"

Branding Directly Influences Growth

If you were in charge of placing orders, and there were two companies offering pretty much the same pricing and quality, what would you base your decision on? If you son or daughter received offers from two companies equal in terms of name value and financial compensation, which offer would you encourage them to accept? I think that most people would probably choose the "better company."

Excellent corporate principles. It values its employees, contributes to society. Has clear goals that it aims to achieve. Furthermore, a clear brand as a company created by these elements. Probably, there are times where you tend to choose the company with the superior brand, even if the price was somewhat higher or if the name value and compensation were somewhat low.

If you want to increase your stakeholders and retain good employees, branding is simply indispensable. Even a major corporation with a proud history will soon lose the affections of its stakeholders if its brand collapses.

You often hear venture companies and SMEs lamenting the fact that they cannot attract talented employees. Due to the impacts of changes in population, a falling birth rate/aging society and a resurgent economy, companies are now vying with each other to get hold of truly talented workers. On another front, there is gradual awareness that young people selecting companies based on name value or by prioritizing stability and compensation – much like the act of selecting a university based purely on your standard score – has robbed the Japanese economy of its vitality. These days, it is certainly not rare to hear of people who focus entirely on polishing their strongest skill at the earliest stage with the aim of working at a company where they can further enhance this niche expertise. There is nothing more appealing than being able to throw yourself into what you want to do straight away, especially when you are young.

If there is no brand, however, how exactly can a company emphasize its appeal to prospective young employees? Branding is mandatory to connect with stakeholders and to retain talented employees. It is branding that determines the growth of a company.

Export Desire, Not Just Quality

Incidentally, as you have noticed, this book has an English parallel translation alongside the Japanese. This is a first for

今回、本文の英語対訳を掲載している。私の著書としては初めての試みだ。海外に出た企業、海外経験の長い日本人なら誰でも知っていることだろうが、実は日本のブランド価値はかなり高い。

日本人の作り出すモノやサービスへの信頼感、アイデアの独創性、そしてライフスタイルや文化、伝統のユニークさまでが、少なからぬ外国人にとって、憧れとリスペクトの対象だ。それを一番知らないのは、むしろ当の日本人自身であると私には思える。

ただ、海外のビジネスパーソンに今までなかなか伝わっていなかったのは、「いったい日本の企業、そして日本で働く人は、どんな『想い』で良質なモノやサービスを提供しているのか」ということだった。これを、日本企業はブランディングに対する努力が総じて不足しているととらえることもできるだろう。確かにその通りだから。ただ私は、同時に、このポイントにこそ、成熟した経済の中で今後も低成長が続くと諦められがちの日本企業が持っている、大きな伸びしろが隠されていると考える。

今回、さまざまな企業の経営者に話を聞いた。読者の中には、わざわざ英語にして海外の読者に訴えなくとも、内需だけで十分持続していけるのではないかと思える企業があったという印象を持っている人もいるだろう。しかし同時に、彼らにはそれぞれ、オリジナリティにあふれた想いや哲学があり、そこからあふれ出るブランドを武器にビジネスを進めてきた企業であることも、十二分におわかりいただけたはずだ。イマジナの考えるブランディングとは、企業価値を高めるための、想いを明確にする作業の援護であるといえる。そして、世界に向けても発信していきたい、というのが、今回の私のチャレンジでもある。

ジャパン・ブランドへの想い

現在、イマジナが東京に拠点を置いて、これから海外に進出しようと考えている、あるいは海外で勝負できると私たちが考える企業を支援している理由の背景には、「ジャパン・ブランド」への想いと可能性があるからだ。

無印良品のブランド化のケースを考えればわかる通り、海外の視点では、日本で成功した事実自体がすでにブランドであり、考え方を説明できれば海外でも十分受け入れられる時代になっているのに、そこに踏み込もうとする企業はまだ多くない。私たちは、これを非常にもったいないことだと考えている。

日本にはほぼすべてといっていいくらいバ

me as an author. While this is well known to companies who have ventured abroad and Japanese people who have long experience abroad, the fact is that the value of Japanese brands are very high.

Trust in products and services created by Japanese people, the ingenuity of ideas, the uniqueness of its traditions, lifestyles and culture – all of these are the object of longing and respect by foreigners, in no small measure. I think that the people most unaware of this fact are Japanese people themselves.

However, something that has not trickled down to foreign businesspersons so far is the question of what exactly is the 'philosophy' behind Japanese companies and their employees being able to provide such superior quality products and services? You could say that in general, Japanese corporations are not making sufficient efforts towards branding; because this is precisely the case. I, however, at the same time believe that it is exactly this point which belies the major growth potential in Japanese companies, which are resigned to the fact that low growth will become the norm in future in an economy that has reached maturity.

This time, I heard the stories of various corporate managers. I am sure that some readers feel that some of these companies can sustain themselves perfectly well through just domestic demand, without the need to translate into English to appeal to overseas readers. However at the same time, I think such readers can also fully appreciate that these respective corporate managers and their companies have their own philosophies and feelings brimming with originality which they have drawn upon to create brands that allowed them to propel their businesses forward. imajina sees branding in terms of providing support for the process of elucidating the philosophy and feeling required for elevating the value of companies. My challenge this time, meanwhile, is to transmit this outward to reach people around the world.

*In Japan, people do not usually use English on a daily basis.

Desire for Japan Brands

Based in Tokyo, imajina supports companies thinking of advancing overseas or companies that we believe can flourish overseas; in the background to doing so is the fact that there is desire and potential for "Japan Brands."

As is evident when you consider the case of MUJI's branding, seen from other countries, the very fact of having succeeded in Japan constitutes a brand; despite the fact that we now live in an era where explaining your philosophy is enough to be accepted overseas, there are not many companies who attempt to do so. We believe that this is a terrible waste.

Japan boasts an abundant variety of high-quality industries. I might even

リエーション豊かな産業が揃い、しかもどのジャンルもクオリティが高い。あえて述べるなら、「無形の価値」を信じ、投資していこうとする考え方に関してだけは、まだまだである。ただ、それだけブランディングの余地が残されている世界都市は他にないとも考えられる。挑戦する価値があるし、なんといっても、日本は私たちの故国だ。頑張ってほしいという素朴な願いがある。インフラ整備、人口や規模、モラルやルール、安全性に至るまで、東京、日本は世界に誇れる水準にある。クオリティはそのままに、経済がグローバル化していく中で、海外の発想を取り入れる柔軟ささえあれば、もっと日本を活性化できる。今、街中に外国人観光客があふれ、しかもリピーターが少なくない事実は、決して単なる円安だけでは説明できない。

ジャパン・ブランドは、日本でしっかりクオリティをコントロールしながら、誇れる仕事を続けている人たちの気持ちを系統立て説明することで、一層強くブランディングできる。そして、日本人だって外から褒められればうれしいし、自国を見直し始める。ここに、私たちイマジナのチャンスとチャレンジの意義はある。

海外で成功している企業の共通点

私たちの経験を振り返ると、海外で成功している日本企業には共通点がある。一口に海外進出と言っても、日本で十分に成功している企業がテスト的に海外に出て行く事例と、本気で海外のマーケットを取りに行く挑戦では、かなり意味合いも様相も異なる。どちらも意味があるビジネスではあるが、より成功に近い形でビジネスを展開できている企業には、「最初から準備万端である」という点が共通している。

海外では、文化も、雇用慣習も、その企業の何が評価され、どこにリスクがあるのかも日本の常識ではあらかじめ判断できない。それがわかっている企業は、初めから海外をよく知る人々と手を組み、周到に準備を行う。しかし、残念なことに、こうした日本企業は多くはない。無形の価値に対する考え方が不足していて、問題が起きてから初めて、専門家を探し始めるのだ。もちろん、予算をはじめとするリソースの問題から、対症療法的にサポートを頼ることも致し方ない面はある。ただ、現地をよく知る私たちには、極めてもったいない事例が少なくない。

「初めから相談してくれれば、トラブルや摩

venture the view that Japan believes in "intangible value," and the inclination to aggressively invest has not yet taken root. However, it is possible that there are no other global cities that still have so much scope for branding left. It is worth the challenge, and when all is said and done, Japan is my native land. It is my simple hope that Japan does the best that it can. In terms of infrastructure, population and scale, morals and rules, safety and security, Tokyo and Japan are world-class. Retaining its high quality, as economies become increasingly globalized, if Japan can be flexible enough to incorporate ideas from other countries, it can be further rejuvenated. These days, foreign tourists line the streets; the fact that many are repeaters is not solely attributable to the weak yen.

Japan Branding, while strictly controlling the quality in Japan, can be further reinforced by systematically explaining the feelings of the people who take such a pride in their work. On being praised by people overseas, Japanese people will happily begin to re-appraise their own country. Herein lies the opportunity and significance of the challenge for imajina.

Commonalities of Companies that Enjoy Success Overseas

Seen through the lens of our extensive experience, there are common features among Japanese companies that succeed abroad. When it comes to overseas expansion, we should distinguish between companies that venture overseas on an experimental basis having already succeeded in Japan, and companies taking up the challenge of trying to conquer the overseas market. While both of these are valid approaches, companies that are well poised to succeed tend to have in common the fact that they are fully prepared from the outset.

In other countries, cultural and employment norms are different, making it impossible to determine in advance what a company will be appreciated for and what the risks will be based on Japanese common sense. Companies who understand this join forces with people well-versed in overseas affairs from the outset, carrying out meticulous preparations. Regrettably, however, such companies are few and far between in Japan. Lacking understanding of intangible value, they only start to look for an expert once problems have materialized. Of course, problems connected to budgets and other resources make relying on stopgap measures unavoidable. With extensive experience in the field, however, all too often we see cases where the whole exercise is a terrible waste.

"If only you had come to us in the first place, we could have prevented the trouble and hassle, and helped you advance abroad in a smooth manner."

擦を未然に防ぎ、よりスムーズにビジネスができたはずなのに」

そんな、忸怩たる思いに沈むこともままあることだ。成功している企業は、決して自社ですべてを賄おうとはしない。留学経験者、語学の使い手がいて、日本における自社のビジネスに精通しているからといって、彼らがそのまま海外進出のエキスパートに横滑りできるわけではないことを、よく知っている。国内の人事ローテーションの一環として、2～3年で安易に異動させるなど、戦い方を知っている企業は絶対にしない。何も難しい話ではない。企業としての想いを伝えられる人に、専門家をセットしておけば、日本企業の成功確率は高い。

ステークホルダーを増やそう

私たちイマジナの仕事の根幹は、ステークホルダーを増やすことだ。それはクライアント企業の市場や規模、そして発想そのものを大きく変えていく事業である。

ある企業があったとしよう。その会社には社員がいる。彼らは自分の属する企業のことをよく知っているし、当然自分たちでその企業のミッションとは何かを考え、コンセプトとしてまとめ上げる力を持っている。ところが、多くの社員は、現在働いている企業と、せいぜいかつて自分がいた企業についてくらいしかわからない。そもそも、知る必要も、知るきっかけもない。ミッションを考える過程にイマジナが関わる意味は、他の何千社という企業で同じ作業に携わってきた点にある。ノウハウと事例の積み重ねがあり、しかも国内だけでなく、海外に進出した日本企業の情報や組み合わせのバリエーションを豊富に持っている。だから、イマジナが加わってある企業のミッションを考えると、その企業の細部や内部を知り尽くしている人にはかえってわからない面を見出すことができる。

たとえば、衰退産業と呼ばれる業界にあって、伸び悩んでいるように見える企業。すばらしい創業者のおかげで長い間事業を継続してきたものの、現在において想いをまとめきれなくなっている企業。日本以外ではビジネスが成立しないと考えている企業。そこで、私たちが360度の眼で見渡すと、新しい市場を開拓できる可能性、新たな成長機会、そして見えなかった社会的価値、ミッションが見出せる。その結果として、これまでになかった角度からのブランディングが可能となる。日本以外にも伝わる企業文化としてもう一度見直し伝えていくことで、国内のみならず海外にもステークホルダー

It is not unusual for us at imajina to feel this sense of chagrin. Companies that are successful never try to cover all bases by themselves. They fully understand that it is simply not feasible to expect that an employee - who has studied abroad or who is good at languages and also well versed in the company's business in Japan – will be able to shift into the role of overseas expansion expert. Companies who understand strategy well never move people around every two to three years as part of their domestic personnel rotation. There is nothing complicated about this. There is a high success rate among Japanese companies who appoint an expert who is capable of communicating the company's philosophy.

Increase Stakeholders

An essential part of our work at imajina is increasing stakeholders. This is a business that significantly transforms the market and scale of our client's companies, as well as bringing about a change in their actual thinking.

Let us say there is a company. In that company are employees. They understand their company very well, and as a matter of course think for themselves about what the mission of the company is, and have the ability to conceptualize this mission. On the other hand, in most cases, company employees only have a basic knowledge of their current company and at the most, about companies where they used to work. To begin with, they do not need to know, and have no opportunity to find out. The significance of imajina getting involved in the stage of thinking about a company's mission is that we have been through this exact process with thousands of other companies. We have accumulated a wealth of know-how and case examples, and not just domestically; as a result, imajina possesses a varied body of information about a range of Japanese companies that it has helped to advance abroad. Thus, when imajina gets involved in conceptualizing a company's mission, we can often uncover aspects that have even eluded someone who knows the inner workings and peculiarities of that company.

For example, a company making little progress in an industry said to be in decline. A company that, despite having remained in business for a long time thanks to a highly capable founder, is no longer able to pinpoint what its philosophy is. A company that thinks it will never be able to establish a business outside of Japan. At such junctures, taking an extensive 360-degree view, we are able to pick out possibilities for cultivating new markets, new growth opportunities and social value, and a mission that had been obscured from view up until then. The result of this is that branding becomes possible from angles that were previously not visible.

が増えていく。良い取引先を呼び込み、良い人材を確保するきっかけになる。

断言するが、こうした流れを無理に内製化することは、かなりもったいない。プロにできること、プロならではのノウハウがある。しかも、ひとつとして同じ企業はない。ブランディングは、すべてがオーダーメイドなのだ。

他者の考えを汲み取るブランディング

今回の書籍の中に、ひとつの通底したテーマがある。それは、イマジナという「他者」による分析が加わることで、それぞれの企業に新しい付加価値、新しいブランディングの可能性を見出してほしい、という想いだ。そして、インタビューを受けてくださった経営者は、一様にそれを好意的に受け止めてくれた。はっきり申し上げて、自動車教習所業界は斜陽だ。だが、武蔵境自動車教習所の例、そしてエーピーアイの例を見れば、ここに「高齢者の安全を確保する」という新しい価値、あるいは「健康産業」としての新しい姿が見えてこないだろうか。

本書でご紹介した経営者は、いずれも努力を欠かさない尊敬できる方々ばかりだ。当然、自社のビジネスが持っている新しい可能性について、日々アンテナを張り巡らせ、最新の情報を収集することに力を惜しまない。それでもなお、自らだけではできないことがあるという事実に対して、彼らは実に謙虚だ。

経営者としての仕事。そして、その結果構築されている現在の自社のブランド。今後のポテンシャル。そうした経営の核心部分について、私たちに対しても隠すことなく、また私たちのような外部の視点を尊重し、汲み取ろうとしてくれる。それは謙虚さであると同時に、健全な貪欲さでもある。自らの魅力、自らの弱点。現在の課題や将来の方向性について、真剣に考えているからこそ、それが「他者からどう見られているか」についても、心を砕くのだ。

他者の考えを汲み取る。これは、ブランディングを考える上での大きなきっかけになると思う。いい企業ほど、それを自社にプラスとなるすばらしい経験と考え、労力を惜しまないのだ。

伝統企業こそブランディングが有効

今回見てきたさまざまなケースの中には、すでに長い歴史を有していて、外部から見れば十二分にブランドを確立できているように見える企業もあった。イマジナは、こうし

Through re-thinking corporate culture into something that can resonate outside of Japan, it is possible to increase stakeholders not only domestically but also overseas. This provides the catalyst for calling in beneficial business partners and for retaining capable personnel.

We can say with absolute certainty that striving to expedite this flow of events in-house is a terrible waste. There are things that professionals can do, and know-how that only professionals have. Furthermore, no two companies are identical. When it comes to branding, everything is order-made and tailor-made.

Branding that Picks Up on Other People's Thinking

There is one underlying theme throughout this book: imajina's desire that through providing analysis as an outside source to each respective company, those companies can discover new possibilities for added value and branding. Each of the corporate managers who kindly agreed to be interviewed took in our analysis obligingly. To be frank, the driving school business is an industry in decline. However, as with the example of Musashi Sakai Driving School and the example of API, we will see the emergence of new value such as "ensuring the safety of the elderly" or a new incarnation in the form of "the health industry."

All of the corporate managers introduced in this book are hard-working people well worthy of our respect. Needless to say, when it comes to new possibilities inherent in their company's business, they spare no effort in keeping an ear to the ground to pick up the latest information. Another feature among them is that they are all genuinely humble about the fact that there are things that they cannot do alone.

Their jobs as corporate managers. Their own-company brands constructed as a result of their work. Future potential. Regarding such crucial elements of their management, they concealed nothing from us, and respected and readily accepted the perspectives provided by an outside source such as imajina. As well as modesty, this also springs from a healthy acquisitiveness. Their own appeal points, their own weaknesses. They think very hard about current issues and future orientation, and because of this, they can also devote themselves to the issue of "how do others see us."

Taking in what other people think. I believe that this is a major catalyst when it comes to thinking about branding. The better the company is, the more willing they are to make an effort to take in other people's points of views because they know it will have a positive effect on their thinking and their company.

た伝統を有する企業も、ブランディングをしっかり行うことでさらなる成長が見込め、一層ポテンシャルを発揮できると考えている。むしろ、創業から日が浅くとも、ブランディングがしっかりしている企業のほうが強いとさえいえる。なぜなら、強い想いとともに創業した経営者が健在で、自らの声で、強くメッセージを発することができる。

しかし、創業から何代も代替わりした企業においては、いったい創業者がどのような想いで立ち上げたのか、どんな方法で社会に貢献してきたのか、そしてこれからどこに向かって進んでいくのかが、かえってぼやけてしまうことがある。すばらしい会社なのに、伝統と歴史があるのに立ち行かなくなる会社には、たいがいこの種の問題が隠れている。それはひとかどの時代を築いた大企業であろうと、例外ではない。

事業をうまく継承している企業は、この点をとてもうまくブランディング、あるいはリブランディングしている。そのヒントは、本書の中にもたくさん隠れている。創業者の想いを現代的に解釈し直すとどうなるのか、将来的な目標に置き換えるとどんな答えが見えてくるのか、時代の変化に合わせて足したり引いたりするべきことはないか、常にメンテナンスを怠らない。これがなければ、どんなに歴史と伝統に惹かれて良い人材を集めてもすぐに流出してしまうだけだ。ブランディングに、企業の歴史の長さは関係ない。言い換えれば、良い企業はどんなケースでも、不断のブランディングを怠ってはいない。

グローバル時代だからこそ、企業理念の「質」が大切

企業が成長し、人的にも規模が拡大していく局面では、得てしてルールとマニュアル、人事制度などに頼り、その精度を高めることで対処しようと考える経営者が多い。それは100％間違いではないのだが、同時に無理も生じやすい。

企業が経営者ひとりでは見きれない規模に成長するタイミングで、あるいは日本で勝負してきたブランドを海外で試す局面で、ルールとマニュアル、報酬制度だけで対処しようとすれば、必ずと言っていいほど歪みを生んでしまう。

「何かあった時」に、対処しきれなくなってしまうからだ。そして、今では対処しきれなかった事実が、あっという間に何倍にも増幅された悪いイメージとして社会に消費され、会社の存続そのものを脅かす事態にまで、あっという間に悪化させてしまうリスクをはらんでいる。グローバルなネット時代において、情報は統制できず、筒抜けなのだ。

It is Traditional Companies that Require Effective Branding the Most

Within the various cases introduced this time, there are companies that already have a long history, and that when observed from the outside, seem to have established their brands to a level that is more than sufficient. We at imajina believe that providing proper branding for these traditional companies will bring them more growth and allow them to realize another level of potential. In some cases, there are companies that despite not having been established very long are stronger than long-established companies because of their solid branding. This is because founder of the company is still at its head and remains able to transmit their strong convictions on the front line.

However, with more traditional companies where the manager has changed again and again over generations since foundation, there tends to be a blurring of vital elements such as the original desire of the founder, how he/she intended to contribute to society, and where the company is headed. This kind of problem tends to be concealed within most companies that flounder despite being wonderful companies with proud traditions and long histories. Companies that built up a fully-fledged era are not exempt from this.

Companies who ably deal with the succession issue are able to successfully implement branding or indeed re-brand. There are many such clues concealed within this book. What would be the result of re-interpreting the founder's desire to the current age? What sort of answers would be gained from realigning future goals? What needs to be added or taken away to align the company to the changes of the era? Such ongoing maintenance cannot be neglected. Without it, capable employees whom you managed to attract through history and tradition will soon drift away. With branding, the length of a company's history is irrelevant. Put another way, good companies must without exception, be unflaggingly vigilant regarding their branding.

The "Quality" of a Corporate Philosophy is Particularly Relevant in a Globalized Era

As companies grow, in the phase where the number of personnel also expands, there are many managers who deem it appropriate to deal with this expansion by simply relying on rules, manuals and personnel frameworks, updating them on an ad-hoc basis. While this is not 100percent misguided, it can also cause extra strain.

When companies start grow to a scale that cannot be overseen by one single corporate manager, or in the phase where brands successful in Japan start

成長の過程で質を確保する場合には、なぜそういったルールなのか、なぜマニュアルをそう定めたのか、人事制度は何を評価しているのかといった根本的な戦略が存在しない限り、いざ何かあった時に、立ち戻る場所がなくなってしまう。これは、企業理念の「質」そのものだ。

私たちは何のために働いているのか、どこを目指しているのか。そうした深い、そして強い想いがなければ、どんなに立派な制度を構築しても、ブランディングにはなり得ないのだ。海外進出でも、それは変わらない。むしろ、国民性と文化的な背景に頼り、不文律によってある程度のモラル確保が期待できる日本国内とは違い、明確な企業理念がなければ、社員の方向性が合うということを期待しにくい。書籍だけでなく、インターネットや映像も駆使して、質の高い想いを伝えていく努力が大切になってくる。社員が企業理念を自分のこととして語れるようになれば、ブランドはどんどん高まっていく。

なぜイマジナは経営コンサルティングをしないのか

イマジナは、映像やネットも手がける一方、紙でできたカルチャーブックにこだわっている。そしてこの本を上梓した理由、あるいは今回の取材と感想をわざわざ本という形でまとめた理由も、実はブランディングの一環である。今どき紙の本など古臭い、もう電子書籍の時代だ、と言う人がいる。では、実際にここまで本書をお読みいただいたあなたはどうだろうか。同じ内容を電子書籍で読んだ場合、あるいはビデオで見せられた場合とでは、印象は異なるのではないだろうか。

イマジナが紙のカルチャーブックを止めない理由、そして私が本書をここまで書いてきた理由は、「紙の本にしかできないことがある」からだ。ネットやテレビと違って安易に読み流したり、聞き流したりできない。新聞や雑誌と違い簡単にゴミ箱に捨てられない。こうした感覚が人々の間に共有されている限り、紙の本を作っていく価値は存在し続ける。よく誤解されるのだが、私たちイマジナは経営コンサルティング会社ではない。あくまで企業ブランディングと、組織、人事制度などに特化している企業だ。

企業が淘汰されていく時代、企業は何によってふるいにかけられているのか。私たちの答えは、「人材に対してどれだけの想いをかけているか」だ。ブランディングで差別化を図り、良い人材を集めることが経営の根幹だと考えている。そしてこれは、恐らく一

to test the waters overseas, trying to cope solely through rules, manuals and compensations systems will definitely result in discord within the company.

The reason for this is that "when something goes wrong," they are unable to fully deal with the problem. Then, in this day and age, the fact that they were unable to resolve the issue soon balloons into a negative image many times worse; this negative image is subsequently absorbed by society, potentially leading to a situation that could threaten the very existence of the company. In the globalized era of the Internet, it is not possible to keep a lid on information, which can leak out completely.

When aspiring to ensure quality in the growth phase, if there is no fundamental strategy specifying why there are rules, why a manual was created in a certain way, what the human resources system is assessing – when things do go awry, there is no point to revert to. This is exactly what the "quality" of corporate principles is.

What are we working for, where are we headed? Without such deep and strong convictions, no matter how sophisticated a system you construct, branding cannot be successfully achieved. The same applies for overseas expansion. In contrast to Japan where there are unwritten rules and a national character and cultural background that everybody shares - which to an extent guarantees a certain level of morals- without clear and precise corporate principles, it is hard to expect employees to all pull in one direction. It is important to go beyond the written word and to make use of the Internet and video to transmit a high-quality philosophy. If employees are able to articulate the company's principles in their own way, the brand can soar to greater heights.

Why Doesn't imajina Offer Corporate Consulting?

While utilizing video and online content to an extent, imajina is focused on culture books printed on paper. The reason for publishing this book, or indeed the reason for going to the trouble of summing up all of the interviews and realizations into this book, is in fact because it constitutes one strand of branding. These days, one sometimes hears people saying that books are out of date, that this is the era of digital books. So, how about you, the reader, who has actually taken the trouble to read this book up until here? Would your impression be different if you had read the same content in a digital publication or if you had seen it on a video?

The reason why imajina does not stop publishing culture books and the reason why I have written this book up until here is because "some things can only be done with paper books." Unlike the Internet and television, you cannot simply skim through it or casually listen.

般的な経営コンサルタントの答えではないだろう。情報が瞬時に共有され、ノウハウの囲い込みが困難な今では、どれだけ新しい業態を開発し、角度をつけたサービスを行おうと、ビジネスとしてうまくいっている事実はあっという間に知れ渡り、法令で保護されていない以上はコピーされる。それは残念なことではあるが、結局絶えず挑戦していくしか解決策はないのだ。

自分より発想力の優れた人材を確保する

今後は、いかに柔軟で豊かで新しい発想を世に問えるかが、企業の実力になってくる。牧歌的な時代であれば、その役目は天才的な経営者がひとりいれば十分だった。だが、現代の勝負はとてもひとりの人間では賄えないほど、あっという間に限界値がやってくる。経営者自身と同じ、あるいは自分より発想力の豊かな人材がいなければ、もはや経営は成り立たない。

この事実を認識している経営者は、より良い仲間集めのための努力を惜しまない。自分の考え、自社のブランドをはっきり打ち出すことが、自社のブランドをより高めてくれる人材を集める最高の方法だとわかっているからこそ、ブランディングに手間とリソースをかけるのだ。

ミッションで響き合う人たちは、いつでも信頼関係で結ばれ、お互いを高めていく。ブランディングとは、その繰り返しなのだ。硬直化した日本の人材事情は大いにゆらぎ、働く人は自らの実力とミッション、そして働きやすさとカルチャーを求めて、一斉に流動し始めた。それは企業にとってピンチでもあり、大きなチャンスでもある。成長する企業は大きく力を伸ばし、衰退する企業はあっという間に消えていく。雇用が動けば、人も企業も成長する。当然、日本も良くなっていく。イマジナの企業ブランディングは、自社の成長だけでなく、日本のすばらしい企業の成長を後押しできる。

ブランディングはそんな時代を生き抜くための手段であり、企業と人、想いと想いを結びつける大切な媒介になる。そんな会社は、幸せを感じる社員であふれるはずだ。

外から「いいね!」と言ってもらおう

サントリーやニッカが長年すばらしいウイスキーを作り続けてきたことは、ファンならば随分前から知っていた事実である。しかし、メジャーなドラマの題材になったことで改めて一般の注目を集め、品切れが続いたこと

Unlike newspapers and magazines, you cannot easily throw it into the trash. As long as this understanding prevails, there will be sufficient value in creating paper books. People often get the wrong end of the stick by assuming that imajina is a management consultancy, which we are not. It should be noted that we are a company that specializes in corporate branding and personnel and organizational systems.

In an era where companies are getting culled, on what basis are they sifted out? Our answer would be "the extent to which their energy is focused on their employees." I believe that the crux of management is to differentiate your company through branding, in order to attract a talented workforce. I would even venture that this would not be the answer given by a typical management consultant. In an age where information is instantly shared, making the retention of know-how somewhat problematic, no matter what how much you develop a new business category and provide service from a new angle, the fact that your business is successful will become common knowledge in no time and will be imitated unless it is protected by law. While this is a shame, ultimately the only solution is to keep on coming up with new ideas.

Securing Personnel with Greater Inventive Powers than Yourself

In future, the extent to which companies can come up with new ideas and flexible, rich concepts will determine their true strength. In an ideal situation, it would be enough for one genius manager to fulfill this role. However, in this day and age it is not possible to succeed with just one leader – their limits would soon become apparent. Without personnel who have inventiveness equal to their manager, or indeed creative power in excess of them, successful management is not possible.

Corporate managers who accept this fact will not cut any corners in striving to attract a higher quality of employee. Precisely because they understand that clearly articulating their ideas and their brand is the ultimate method for attracting employees capable of taking their brand to even greater heights, they are quite happy to expend time and resources on branding their company.

A group of people who march together under the same mission will always be bonded by a relationship of trust, and will continue to mutually elevate one another. Branding is the repetition of this. Japan's rigid personnel system is starting to crumble, precipitating a torrent of working people gravitating towards more reasonable working cultures that better reflect their true abilities and their own personal missions. This is a crunch for companies, but also presents a major opportunity. Companies that

は記憶に新しい。実は日本のウイスキーが海外の本場から極めて高い評価を受けていたことが評価されたのだ。私はここに、ふたつの似て非なるポイントを見る。

外から「いいね!」と言ってもらえると、人はより鮮明に反応するということだ。ひとつは、ドラマというギミック。もうひとつは、ウイスキーの本場英国での評価。もしこれが、さほど視聴率の高くないバラエティ番組での紹介で、しかも国内での評価であったとしたら、仮にウイスキーそのものの中身はまったく同一であっても、評価はまったく違っただろう。

私は繰り返し日本が作り出すモノとサービスのすばらしさを説いてきたが、ブランド化していくためのひとつの方法は、どうやって外からの「いいね!」を集めるかにかかってくるのではないかと思う。そしてキラーコンテンツになるのは、日本が近代化を学んだ欧米での評価だ。

無印良品が「MUJI」としてニューヨークやロンドン、パリやミラノに展開されているのを現地で目の当たりにした時、得も言われぬ感動に襲われる。帰国してからも、無印良品を見る眼が変わっていることに気づく。無印良品は昔からすばらしいブランドであり、筋の通ったライフスタイルを提案し続けていることはすでに紹介した通りだが、いとも簡単に魔法にかかってしまう。大昔の伊万里焼だって浮世絵だって、実は同じことなのだ。

中小企業でも、内需系企業でも関係ない。私は、日本で頑張ってきた企業にこそ、無印良品の後に続いてほしいと願う。イマジナは、その支援を企業ブランディングという側面から頑張りたいと心から願っている。

grow will further extend their power, while companies in decline will soon disappear. If employment starts to shift, people and companies grow with it. Japan will of course take a turn for the better. Thus, imajina's corporate branding is not solely for the growth of individual companies, but also exists to provide a tail wind for the growth of Japan's excellent companies.

Branding is a means of surviving such an era, and as such is a precious medium for linking people with companies, and linking desire with desire.
Such companies are bound to be full to the brim with contended employees.

Getting People Outside to Click the "like" Button

The fact that Suntory and Nikka have made superb whisky for many years is nothing new to their fans. However, it is only relatively recently that they came to be known by the general public after featuring in a major drama, after which they simply flew off the shelves. In fact, Japanese whisky was held in high regard for having received extremely high recognition in countries known to be the homes of whisky around the world. Within this, I see two points that are similar but also different.

In general, people react more vividly if they hear "that is great" from someone outside. One element of this is the gimmick that is drama. The other is, being held in high regard in the UK, the home of whisky. If it had been featured on a non-prime time Japanese entertainment TV program and highly rated within Japan, the evaluation would be completely different even if it were exactly the same whisky.

Over and over again, I have extolled the virtues of services and products made in Japan; yet I believe that one method for rendering these into brands is directly linked to getting people outside japan to "like" the greatness of these products and services. To become truly awesome products, they will need to be recognized and valued in the West, the place Japan emulated in its quest for modernization.

I always feel so impressed when I see MUJI stores when I am walking down the street in New York, London, Paris or Milan; when I come back to Japan I can see the company from a different perspective. I have already introduced the fact that MUJI has for a long time been a wonderful brand that have continued to propose logical, rational lifestyles – its magic is irresistible. In fact it is the same phenomenon as Imari porcelain or ukiyoe paintings centuries ago.

Whether the company is an SME or a domestically-focused company, it makes no difference. I want companies who battled hard in Japan to follow in MUJI's footsteps. imajina genuinely aspires to provide support in the form of corporate branding. This is our fervent hope.

[著者]

株式会社イマジナ 代表取締役社長
関野吉記　Yoshiki Sekino

London International School of Acting卒業。イマジネコミュニカツオネ入社。サムソナイトなど多くのコマーシャル、映画製作を手がける。その後、投資部門に出向し、アジア統括マネージャーなどを歴任する。

経営において企業ブランディングの必要性を痛感し、2006年、株式会社イマジナを設立。2000社以上のブランディングやHRコンサルティングを行っている。同社代表取締役社長。その他にも多くの企業の役員を兼任し、ブランディングからの企業再生を続けている。

2012年には国連WAFUNIF(国連共同教育派遣協会)の代表理事に就任。人づくりによる社会貢献を目指し、教育、育成、ボランティア活動を続けている。

株式会社イマジナ 代表取締役
（社）国連共同教育派遣協会 PR大使
奥山由実子　Yumiko Okuyama

東京、浅草出身。1993年、米国に人事コンサルティング会社（本社・ニューヨーク）を設立。1,500社にのぼる在米日系企業に数々の人事管理プロジェクトを提言。日本企業としての独自性を尊重しながら、世界標準の人事システムの導入を推薦し、経営の高度化と人的資源の活性化、人事トラブルの解決と防止などに大きな役割を果たしてきた。

こうしたノウハウ、クライアント企業からの熱い信頼と支援のもと、2006年6月、関野とともにイマジナを設立。企業カルチャーブランディング構築、評価制度設計、報酬戦略の立案、グローバル人材研修など、多岐にわたるサービスを提供している。

世界で勝てるブランディングカンパニー
ブランド力でマネジメントを強化する日本企業の挑戦

2015年12月17日　第1刷発行
2017年11月22日　第2刷発行

著者	関野吉記／奥山由実子
発行所	ダイヤモンド社 〒150-8409 東京都渋谷区神宮前6-12-17 http://www.diamond.co.jp/
電話	03-5778-7235（編集）　03-5778-7240（販売）
ブックデザイン	森田恭行＋高木瑶子（キガミッツ）
翻訳	ジョエル・チャレンダー（Joel J L Challender）
制作進行	ダイヤモンド・グラフィック社
印刷	信毎書籍印刷（本文）・共栄メディア（カバー）
製本	加藤製本
編集担当	梶原一義

©2015 Yoshiki Sekino ／ Yumiko Okuyama
ISBN 978-4-478-06668-3
落丁・乱丁本はお手数ですが小社営業局宛にお送りください。送料小社負担にてお取替えいたします。
但し、古書店で購入されたものについてはお取替えできません。
無断転載・複製を禁ず　Printed in Japan